OUTSIDE

Looking In

BRETT CRAWFORD

OUTSIDE
Looking In

A Division of WINEPRESS PUBLISHING

Pleasant Word (a division of WinePress Publishing, PO Box 428, Enumclaw, WA 98022) functions only as book publisher. As such, the ultimate design, content, editorial accuracy, and views expressed or implied in this work are those of the author.

Unless otherwise noted, all Scriptures are taken from the King James Version of the Bible.

Soft Cover:
ISBN 13: 978-1-4141-1114-8
ISBN 10: 1-4141-1114-2

Hard Cover:
ISBN 13: 978-1-4141-1115-5
ISBN 10: 1-4141-1115-0

Library of Congress Catalog Card Number: 2007907116

This book is dedicated to my family and friends mentioned throughout. Special thanks to God for letting me remember the events, for giving me the patience and desire to sit in front of the computer long enough to get them written, and for showing me a relationship between my experiences and his Word. Special thanks to Jan for her criticism. If you think it reads hard now, you should have read some of the stories before she told me they didn't make sense. I wish she would have had time to correct them all. Special thanks to Mama who gave valuable insight when I was stuck on a biblical reference. Special thanks to Daddy, Granny Westmoreland, Barry Crawford, Scott Hatcher, David Tutor, Gary Higgins, Mitch Montgomery, and all the other contributors to my memories that I cherish the most.

Thank you all!

CONTENTS

TOPICAL CONTENTS BY CHAPTER

For the fisherperson – 2, 16, 17, 21, 23, 24, 26, 32, 33, 35, 36, 40, 42, 43, 48, 49, 51, 62, 82, 86, 89, 92, 96, 98, 106

For the rabbit hunter – 15, 57, 60, 74

For the bird hunter – 1, 3, 4, 22, 31, 50, 55, 58, 78, 80, 97, 107

For the chef – 8, 27, 41, 61, 108

On the farm – 6, 12, 34, 38, 46, 47, 52, 66, 69, 100

Other – 11, 13, 14, 18, 45, 53, 59, 63, 64, 65, 70, 85, 91, 94, 95, 99, 105

INTRODUCTION

In late 2002, we were having a lot of trouble with keeping order in our 4th grade Sunday school class. We had a really rambunctious group of boys and girls. The boys were the ones that were difficult to keep in line. I knew this group was coming because I had watched them come up through the preschool department. I had thought about dropping out of teaching Sunday school before they got to my class but decided against it because I did not want a first-time teacher scarred for life and never wanting to teach again. After much prayer and head scratching, God gave me a way to get and keep their attention. If I could relate their lesson to a previous hunting or fishing experience, they seemed to be mesmerized. Sometimes I start a lesson with one and sometimes I would promise them one at the end of class. Sometimes I wasn't able to relate it to the lesson, but the mere thought of it would make them listen to the lesson in anticipation of hearing a hunting story.

After reading through Rick Warren's *40 Days of Purpose*, I thought that someone else could use these stories to help develop their own Sunday school plan. My kids will also appreciate these stories years from now. I still use a story every once in a while in Sunday school but I think God may have let me have a lot of these experiences just for this particular class.

If you were in the 4th grade at West Heights Baptist Church in Pontotoc, MS in 2002, I hope you remember some of the lessons that go along with these stories. The hand signs and facial expressions won't be there but the thoughts are.

Sincerely,
Brett

Chapter 1

DOVE HUNTING –
THE BODY SERVES

A buddy of mine and I were out riding around one afternoon looking for a place to dove hunt. We saw a couple of doves fly over the railroad tracks just south of Algoma, MS. We parked and loaded our shotguns, and walked out into the hay field and jumped a few birds. We harvested two or three. At the sound of the gunshot, I was reminded of the Tarzan movies where the birds started getting up in the African landscape and almost darkened the sky. The doves did not blacken the sky, but there were thousands that flew up off the hayfield and the adjacent wheat field. We spread out and began hunting. We bagged a few more doves, but quickly found that we could not keep them from lighting on the other side of the field well out of range. That evening, we called everyone we could think of and had a great hunt the next day.

> Just as on this field each person was needed (even just to shoot, no matter they couldn't hit anything), God expects us to use our gifts in the church, 1 Corinthians 12:1-30. "As we have opportunity, we must work for the good of all, especially for those who belong to the household of faith."
>
> —Galatians 6:10

Chapter 2

FISHING
IN THE DELTA –
ANXIETY

A couple of friends and I went fishing on a river in the MS delta. When we got there the only place we could find to put the boat into the river was down a cliff next to the road. Against our better judgment we went ahead and put the boat in the water which was rather easy considering how much higher the road was than the river. The river was flowing very fast, which made trot lining very difficult. I kept thinking the line was too tight and would break and rip a few hooks through our hands. It was a very unsuccessful fishing trip. The normal mood of relaxing while fishing was overcome by the anxiety of how we were going to get the boat out of the river. After much effort and moving about three to six inches at a time, we managed to get the boat back up to the road.

Sometimes the anxiety of visiting or witnessing to someone can destroy our day or week.

"Take therefore no thought for the morrow: for the morrow shall take thought for the things of itself. Sufficient unto the day is the evil thereof."

—Matthew 6:34

Chapter 3

CHET'S FIRST DOVE –
THE MARK

One time we went dove hunting below Bruce on my nephew's land next to the Indian burial mound. There was a spot that was too low and stayed wet most of the year. The mound itself would not grow anything (I have no idea why). Around the dove field was my nephew's cotton crop. We had quite a few doves coming in that morning. I would shoot only after my son took the first shot with his 410 single barrel shotgun. After he had shot a couple of boxes of shells, a dove came down the field from right to left flying right along the edge of the cotton field. After Chet squeezed the trigger, the bird was obviously hit. Instead of the common thud of the bird hitting the ground or the helicopter spiral down to the earth, the bird looked like an airplane that had just lost one engine.

As I watched the bird knowing it could be Chet's first, he sailed into the cotton patch about four or five hundred yards away. I marked the bird by a tree in the distance and the number of rows into the cotton patch. I started walking without taking my eyes off the spot where the bird fell. A couple of hundred yards into the walk the thought crossed my mind that I had already bagged a few birds that were easily accessible in case I didn't find his. My thinking shamed me. When I got to where I thought the bird was, I spotted him and quickly rushed back to congratulate my son.

When Peter stepped out of the boat to walk toward Jesus, he had his eye on the mark. The wind and the waves soon distracted him.

Chapter 4

DUCK HUNTING -

SACRIFICE

Once we were duck hunting in the Skuna river bottom. The water had just come up several inches because of the rain. It was considerably higher than normal. We had a few ducks come in, but not enough to keep our eyes glued to the sky. In watching and looking around we noticed what looked like little upside down floating bird nests. There were several around. Closer examination revealed the nests were not nests at all, but floating piles of Fire Ants. Evidently, the water had come up into their nests and forced them out. Instead of spreading out the ants clung together.

Thinking back, I can't help but wonder about the ants on the bottom of the pile. I think it is safe to say that they gave their lives to save the colony. Maybe on purpose, maybe not!

Christ gave his life willingly to save the colony. We have a choice whether to climb on his back and move up out of the water or go down under in our sin. John 3:16, "For God so loved the world that he gave his only begotten son so that whosoever believeth in him should not perish but have everlasting life."

Chapter 5

DEER CAMP (THE GROWN UP YEARS) – *TRIALS*

A few years ago, my cousin and I decided to take our boys and stay the night at our deer camp. We had a mobile home in Calhoun County close to the game management area. We went early and hunted until after dinner. The hunt was enjoyable but fruitless. We decided to go early to our camp so we could work on any water leaks we might have from the previous winter. We fixed a few leaks, but did not have the right fittings for all of them. We also found that the water heater element had gone bad, because we turned the power on before we filled the water heater with water.

One of us went to town and picked up the parts, while the other thawed out deer meat to cook for supper. We were getting excited because eating is the best thing about deer camp. No shortcuts are taken for the meals—homemade biscuits, fried tenderloin, and milk gravy. One of my uncles always said, "You have to eat deer if you want to harvest deer." It always seemed to me it should be the other way around.

We made the repairs and started getting ready to cook. However, the gas tank was empty which meant the stove would not work. Even worse, the heaters would not work, and the temperature was about thirty-five degrees inside and outside the camp. We also found the meat was freezer-burned and did not smell very good. We decided to go through town, eat supper, and then go home. We did not think the boys needed to be in this kind of weather with no heat. At least, that is what we told ourselves as the rain started (almost sleeting). We loaded up everything and started to back out to the highway when I noticed that my truck had a flat rear tire. After we got that fixed we had an enjoyable meal and an uneventful trip home.

> Sometimes when I think nothing else can go wrong and then it does, I am reminded of Job and the hardships that he endured. God allows us all to be in situations we would rather not be in. How we respond to those situations is our choice. We always have a choice! After Job found out he had lost most of his family he said, "Naked came I out of my mother's womb, and naked shall I return thither: the Lord gave and the Lord hath taken away: blessed be the name of the Lord."
>
> —Job 1:21

Chapter 6

THE RIDE -
FITTING IN

We had a saddle horse named Midnight. He was black with a long flowing mane and an unusually wide neck that made him seem a lot bigger while riding him than he really was. One day we were riding in my Granny's back pasture. We came to a small pond that I decided to ride through on Midnight. I had seen people go through the water a lot in westerns and thought I should be able to do it as well. You go into the deep water and then slide off the back and hold to the saddle horn. Simple, right? When we started into the water it was obvious that the horse did not want to go.

When he got about knee deep he decided that he would rather just lie down as swim through this pond and so he did. I managed to keep my leg from getting caught under him as he went down. The second try gave the same results. I changed my mind instead of him changing his.

Sometimes we do things just to be like everyone else. We must be a light in the world but be careful where we try to fit in. Jesus went to eat a meal with Zacchaeus knowing this was against the rules for good Jews. In doing so, salvation came to the house of Zacchaeus.

—Luke 19:1-10

Chapter 7

ANTELOPE –
FIND YOUR GIFT

Charles Roye, Allen Roye, J.D. Adams, and I went to Wyoming antelope hunting. We stayed at a motel in Kaycee Wyoming, where we had trouble with the toilet. I was chosen to go to the office and get a plunger. I put on my camo coat and headed out. On the way back down the street some guy yelled out his window, "Carry that weapon with pride soldier."

On this trip we had almost every kind of weather imaginable: hot, cold, wind, and snow. We saw a lot of antelope, but the only thing I harvested was a groundhog. Antelope can run like the wind and jump when forced. Amazingly, they don't like to jump fences. One of the guys harvested an antelope on a fence row. They had dropped me out a mile or two up the draw. I walked toward them and the antelope ran along the fence until it came past them. I guess they look for places to go under the fence instead of jumping over.

I am sometimes amazed in the church when people do not try things they are very capable of doing. We kind of ease along the fence until we can find a hole to go under and we don't even try. I dare say that many of us haven't tried enough things to know that we have a gift.

One of the guys and I were shooting at a herd of antelope that we had stalked. This has to be done under cover, because their eyes are amazing in the open range. One of them fell. As he was field dressing the antelope, the milk bag burst and sprayed up into his mouth. I didn't taste it, but by the description, it must have been awful. Milk is usually very good.

In Genesis chapter 3, the Bible says the forbidden fruit was pleasant to the eyes. I wonder if it tasted as good as it looked?

Chapter 8

GRILLING SQUIRRELS – WORK IN THE CHURCH

I harvested a couple of squirrels one day and decided to cook them on the grill inside the fireplace. Dad had made a small grill out of expanded metal. We would let the fire burn down and then insert the grill for cooking. We usually cooked quail with a little Worcestershire, butter, salt, and pepper. That was really good. A few days before, I had barbecued some rabbit that turned out excellent. I thought I would cook the squirrels like the rabbit. When I finished cooking and started eating, the meat had a whang to it like no other. It didn't taste very good at all. I kept eating it, because I cooked it and I thought it must be better than what it initially seemed. When I finished the two rodents, the aftertaste was as bad as the initial taste. To this day I have never eaten another barbecued squirrel.

Have you ever seen anyone do something they *thought* was the right thing for the church family (of course not you or me, but someone else!)? It is obvious to everyone that this activity is not in the best interest of those involved, nor is it good for bringing lost people to Christ. Why do we do it anyway?

Chapter 9

LUNCH HUNT - PREPARATION

One day, the HR manager, the materials manager, the engineering manager, and I went to my Granny's at lunchtime to walk a cutover and try to jump a deer. It was only five minutes away. When we drove to the bottom, we noticed a buck in the back corner of the hayfield. We climbed out of the truck and got ready to shoot. We had three rifles and decided to shoot on the count of three. I was propped on the hood, Jamie leaned on the passenger side door, and Walker was sitting on the tailgate propped on the bed of the truck. The deer looked like about a six point and was two hundred and fifty to three hundred yards away. At the end count, Jamie shot once, I shot three times, and Walker only clicked because he had forgotten to load his gun. The deer got away unhurt.

Shooting a deer with an unloaded gun is kind of like teaching a Bible lesson without preparing. "Thy word have I hid in mine heart, that I might not sin against thee."

—Psalm 119:11

Chapter 10

LOST IN NEW HOPE –
THE BIBLE

A group of family members went deer hunting at New Hope. Mike, Marty, David, LD, and myself decided to walk some cutover on the back side of a lake in the New Hope community. We parked beside a big watershed lake and had to get around it to get to the clearcut. When we came to the backwaters we had trouble getting across without the water going over our boots. We walked a few logs and had to carry my nephew, David, part of the way (he was only seven or eight-years-old at the time). We made it across and began to walk the cutover.

This is how we usually walk cutover. Depending on how many people there are for the hunt, we spread out and surround a small block of land. A few of us walk through the hollows and try to make the deer run out the other side. There are many variations of this method. It can even be done alone but is much trickier to get a shot.

Another very important part is making sure everyone knows where everyone else is and who and where the walkers are going.

On this particular walk, I think we saw two deer but no one got a shot. When we started to go back we made a bad decision. We decided to go around the backwaters through a pine thicket of fifteen to twenty-foot tall pines. Obviously, it is difficult to see very far ahead in this type forest. We walked for a long time, intrigued by the unusual amount of buck sign along the way. Part of the walk was down on our knees because of the amount of undergrowth.

We realized we were lost when we came upon a stream that was running the opposite direction of what it should or so we thought. We thought it should be running toward the lake. Being lost is a bad feeling but is calmed considerably when your family is with you. We assumed the creek was running downhill and followed it to a line of trees and then went out to a gravel road and caught a ride to the lake where our vehicle was. I don't know that I have ever heard more moaning and groaning about getting carried because he was so tired as I did from David. I guess if I could have talked someone into carrying me, I would have tried.

If any one of us would have had a compass, we would have been all right. But even with a compass, you have to have a starting direction and/or a reference point. A compass always directs us north. The Bible should be our compass always directing us toward Jesus.

Chapter 11

THE BED –

FAITH

Seven years ago when my daughter was only a few months old, we went camping at Davis Lake. We had a wonderful time cooking, eating, and sharing with friends. We set up a tent in a fairly level area. We did not worry about the ground very much, because we had an air mattress. The temperature got down close to freezing during the night. We were warm and comfortable—my wife, my son, my daughter and I on the mattress. I guess it was loaded enough that my wife decided to let a little air out during the night. She did not fare very well at getting the plug back in the mattress. The next morning we were wishing that we had taken more time to move the sticks and gravel around underneath the tent.

Have you ever wondered about the kind of mat that the man with the palsy was on when his friends let him down into the house in Capernaum where Jesus was? It might have been a bag full of straw. Had we known that our mattress was leaking down to the hard ground, our emotions would have been quite different from the man going down to meet with Jesus. Mark 2:5 states that Jesus saw the faith of this man's friends. One glad day in heaven I want to talk with the sick man to find out if he had faith also, or if his friends talked him into going to see Jesus.

Chapter 12

DIRT CLOD BROTHERS

When we were little, my brother and I used to play down the road from the house at the shop where my granddad and my dad kept all their farming equipment. One particular morning, my brother was down the hill from the shop playing in the dirt next to the road. We had been watching the Olympics and had both been trying the discus and the shot-put with dirt clods. Since my brother had a shiny blond head, it looked like a good target to shoot for but seemed way out of range. I found a dirt clod that was shaped sort of like a discus and began my windup. I wasn't sure how many turns I was supposed to make so I made enough to get a little dizzy and then let it go. It almost looked like it was flying through the air in slow motion. When that red clay clod hit my brother's blond head,

27

it disintegrated and looked like smoke rising from his hair. The race was on to tell Mama. I had to catch him before he got there.

Have you ever thought about the animosity that Joseph's brothers had for him? It is hard for me to imagine. "And when his brethren saw that their father loved him more than all his brethren, they hated him and could not speak peaceably unto him" Genesis 37:4. My brother, sister, and I like to act like the other ones are loved more and treated better. But we know it is not so. Since I have not experienced this kind of favoritism with my siblings, I find it difficult to understand the hatred Joseph's brothers had for him.

Chapter 13

BUZZARD HUNTING – CLEANSING

Snow and ice caused school to be out for a few days. For lack of anything better to do, we decided to go buzzard hunting. I had a 22-rifle, my friend, David Tutor, had a 12-gauge, and my brother, Barry, had a 20-gauge. We walked to the back pasture where we knew there was a buzzard roost; it was a big dead tree where a bunch of buzzards usually stayed. When we got close, there was a buzzard that came over way too high for us to shoot. But we shot at it anyway. We unloaded on it and reloaded and unloaded again. The bird started circling like a helicopter and slowly coasted to the ground. Upon closer examination, we found that the bird had a wingspan of five or six feet. It looked huge. We were surprised to find that there was only a very small body inside all those feathers. We talked Barry into carrying it home so that we could show everyone. After a little while of carrying the gun and the bird, Barry decided it wasn't worth dragging home. We decided we could cut the bird's foot off and prove that we had shot a buzzard. So we took the foot home.

> Hindsight sheds light on the lack of wisdom in buzzard hunting. Buzzards are one of God's ways of cleansing the earth. They eat dead animals. They have an amazing sense of smell. God wanted to cleanse the earth when he sent the flood. He saved Noah and his family, but no one else was spared.

Chapter 14

RIBBON SERPENT

Once when I was at my Granny Crawford's, my cousins and I had been playing down in the bottom of the pasture. I decided to go back to Granny's and get something to eat. As I was walking back along a trail, I noticed a thin black shoestring on the trail in front of me. I reached down to pick it up. As I did, it began to slither off rather quickly. I was stunned. I was so scared that I ran all the way to my Granny's.

Can you imagine Moses thoughts as God turned his staff into a serpent? Do you suppose he was afraid? Exodus 4:3 says that Moses fled from before the serpent. Then he obeyed God and reached and picked it up and it turned back to a staff.

Chapter 15

TRUCK THROUGH THE LAKE –
SIN RATIONALIZATION

B ack when we were rabbit hunting every chance we
got, we went to Grenada one weekend. The place
where we liked to hunt was close to the lake. It had
big swamp rabbits and hillbillies. The lake sometimes
covered part of the road west of Calhoun City. When
we got there, the water was up and covering part of
the road. We reviewed and pondered and made a bad
decision. We could see the road on the other side of the
water several hundred yards away, so it didn't look too
bad. We were in Mitch Montgomery's Bronco and my
brother's Chevy pickup. As we started driving through
the water, it kept getting deeper and deeper. Soon we
were reaching out the side window and waving in the
water with our hands. The water was quickly coming up
to our feet inside the truck. Then the Bronco went dead.

Panicking, we drove on up to the back of the Bronco and tried to push it. When we came out the other side and caught our breath we realized the value in going to the other side was not worth the risk involved in going through the water. Several things could have happened: our trucks could have been ruined (we thought one of them was); we could have run off a washed out bridge, not being able to see the side rails; we could have been stuck in the water with no way to get help.

Sometimes we allow sin to lull us to sleep about the consequences. We either think there are no consequences or they are minimal compared to the physical joys of sin. Most of the time there is a gradual rationalization in our minds that what we are doing or contemplating is not that bad. We should evaluate situations or circumstances before we get so caught up in them that our reasoning is compromised.

Chapter 16

FISHING IN THE STORM – *PETER ON THE WATER*

Once we were out at the Kemp's Watershed Lake fishing for bream on their pontoon boat. My wife, kids, mom, dad, brother, sister-in-law, and niece were all on the boat fishing. We were catching a few very large bream. The weather was overcast but not really alarming. The wind started to pick up so we decided to use the trolling motor to head back a little closer to the trucks. As we started that way, the wind seemed to be blowing hard enough that the trolling motor would not move the pontoon boat .The clouds began to boil and darken. The trolling motor was not helping. The wind pushed us further back into the backwaters of the lake. As we were trying to decide if swimming with a rope pulling the boat would help us, torrents of rain began to fall. The thunder and lightning discouraged us from getting into the water. Everyone was trying to get under the awning in the middle of the boat. My dad was helping the kids get under one of the seats—there was a storage place under the seats for life jackets and such. We started to relax when we realized there was nothing we could do to help our situation. The storm raged on for about twenty or thirty minutes and then it disappeared almost as fast as it had arrived. We were all wet, but no one was hurt.

Going through the storm together seems to bring us a little closer to the ones in the storm with us. Storms also usually remind us of the awesome power of Almighty God.

Our situation had some similarities to Peter's when he walked on the water towards Jesus in Matthew 14:28-31. There was first the storm. Then came the calm when Peter saw the Savior. Calmness came to us when we realized we couldn't control our situation. In Peter's case, he was intent on getting to Jesus, but allowed to storm to distract his focus.

Chapter 17

BOAT WRECK
APRIL 1 –
GOOD SAMARITAN

A few years ago Scott Hatcher (Hatch), Mitch Montgomery, and I went bass fishing on the Tombigbee Waterway. It was April 1st and a very cool morning. Hatch had a very nice fiberglass bass boat that we used for fishing and skiing. We fished for a while and caught four or five bass. I don't remember who caught the biggest or the most, but it doesn't seem very important looking back.

As we were leaving to go home, Hatch was driving and going back and forth across the waterway checking the depth finder. I had a hooded sweatshirt on and had my head down trying to keep warm. I heard Hatch yell and looked up to see the large white rocks of the bank fast approaching on our left. We had banked right trying to get turned back into the waterway. The boat hit the rocks and went airborne! A clockwise roll landed the boat bottom up about fifteen feet out in the water. When I got out from under the boat, Hatch was going up onto the bank where Mitch was waiting. He said I reminded him of Rambo coming out of the water (from speed of exit not physical appearance).

By the time I got out of the water, Hatch was sitting on the rocks with Mitch in his arms. Mitch's face had turned white and something was oozing out of the top of his head. We looked around for the nearest place to call an ambulance and saw a bridge. I took off running and ran about a mile to a small white house where an older lady let me use the telephone. After calling the ambulance, I sat down on the front porch and decided that my leg was broken. Then I thought that there was no way I could have run that far with a broken leg—it must be bruised. I poured the water out of my knee high rubber boots and waited for the ambulance. When we got back to Mitch, he was looking a little better. They put him on a stretcher and we carried him up the hill. At the hospital, they shaved part of his head, put some stitches in, and kept him overnight. Hatch's chest was bruised from where the boat came down on him. But we were all okay.

One of the guys helping us carry the stretcher asked if we were messing with Mary Jane. It was a drug reference. There were no drugs or alcohol involved! I had to be told later what he was talking about. When at the hospital, we called Mitch's mom: "Mrs. Betty, I know you think we are going to pull an April fool joke, but this is not one!"

The next day we went back and got the boat. Someone had dragged it upside down to Crow's Neck. The water was very cold but we managed to get the boat turned over and loaded up. The keys to Hatch's truck were still under the seat and all of our fishing equipment had been recovered the day before. It was a terrible accident, but just not time for any of us to go.

Hatch said that while waiting for the ambulance a boat came by and someone waved, but never offered to stop and help. The river or the waterway was probably one hundred and fifty to two hundred feet wide. Our boat was upside down at the edge of the water. Mitch and Hatch were on the edge of the water in what should have appeared to be obvious distress. Maybe the guys had a scanner and knew that we had help on the way (probably not).

When the priest and the Levite passed by the wounded man (that the good Samaritan later helped), do you think they waved and acknowledged his existence or just passed on by and acted like they did not see him?

—Luke 10:29-37

Chapter 18

SKIING IN THE POND – TEMPTATIONS

One of our friends had acquired a flat bottom fishing and duck hunting boat with a twenty-five horsepower motor. Naturally, we had to try skiing behind it. We put it in the one-acre pond behind my Granny's house. Skiing was fun but to slalom you had to start on two skis and then drop one. We tried starting from the pier. You could sit on the pier, back the boat up to the pier, throttle the boat wide open, and jump just before the slack was all out of the rope. If it didn't jerk your arms out of the sockets, the water wouldn't even go over your knees before you were skiing. Dad made us stop, because the waves were washing the levy away. We moved to a watershed lake south of town. It was a slightly bigger lake but had lots of stumps and dead trees in it. As we were skiing we had to dodge the stumps. One time I had a bad fall and wasn't sure what the problem was until I stood up and was only in ankle deep water.

> Dodging stumps in a lake could be compared to dodging the temptations that Satan throws in our direction. There is no fine line. It is more like a gray area that divides between being in the world as a witness to others and avoiding all appearance of evil. We could have avoided the chances of getting hurt in the stump-ridden lake by not going at all. But think of the fun we would have missed. We can avoid some worldly temptations by only associating with our Christian brothers and sisters. But how do we introduce people to Christ without associating with them?

Chapter 19

SNAKE ON A LOG – *RECOGNIZE*

Once we were going hunting at Noxubee on the refuge. We had a place we liked to hunt which required us to walk a log across the Noxubee River. That is one reason we liked to hunt there, because not many people went to the trouble of crossing the river to hunt. It was only about forty or fifty feet across, and the terrain was flatland with huge old growth hardwoods. The river also twisted like a snake, so it was very easy to get turned around. If you walked up to the river and it was flowing in a different direction than what you thought, most of the time it just meant you had walked up into a loop. If you walked far enough you could find a tree as big as a sidewalk to walk across. Most of the time we did not walk far enough. We would find the nearest snag going across (precarious or not) and go.

One particular day, my friend and I decided to walk across a log that went under the water before it got to the other side. As we got down into the water about ten feet from the other side, we noticed a large Cottonmouth curled up on a log a few feet upstream of where we were going. We realized if it fell off its log our paths would cross, because we were standing on a slippery log with the water rushing past. We quickly decided to back up and hunt up the river a little further before we crossed at a different point.

> Sometimes things are there for us that we just don't see; these could be evil or a gift. When Paul persecuted the Christians, he did not realize what he was doing until he met Jesus personally, Acts Chapter 9.

Chapter 20

BEAVER DAM CROSSING – SCOPE SET

Once I was deer hunting at Sarepta with one of my friends. We split up and I went across a large bottom with a creek on one side. I had to cross a beaver dam to get to the other side of the creek. I hunted for a while with no success and started back. I probably left a little earlier than I normally would, because I was anxious to get back across the dam.

When I started across, I slipped and fell. I caught myself and got only slightly wet, but banged my gun against the wood sticks of the dam. I was using a .270 semiautomatic rifle with a Bushnell scope. The scope had see-through mounts, which meant you could shoot using the scope or look under it and use the iron sights of the rifle. Anytime you bump your scope, the wise thing to do is to immediately bench check it to make sure it is still sighted in correctly. I usually don't do that; I figure the odds are that I won't see anything anyway. Why not enjoy the hunt and take care of it sometime later? If you harvest a deer, then you are just going to have to do a lot of work to get it properly cared for anyway. That kind of goes along with the following logic: "I wasn't going to shoot one, because I was too far from the truck; I didn't want to drag it back."

When crossing the creek, I had noticed a large hornet's nest. The nest was about one-and-a half feet in diameter and hanging from a tree limb. When I got a couple hundred yards away from it, I decided to take a shot at it. It had a hill for a backstop, so it was not an unsafe thing to do. Two or three shots later there was no sign that I had hit the nest. I did not go back and check to see if I had hit it (those of you familiar with hornets understand why). But I did check my scope before the next hunt.

> If my entire purpose in hunting was to harvest game, then it would have been ridiculous for me to keep hunting with a gun that I was not sure was properly set. If you are not sure what is in store for you when this life is over, then you should check your settings. God offers us eternal life as a free gift (John 3:16, 17). It is our responsibility to accept it.

Chapter 21

FISHING WITH MILFY AT BIG OWL – PERSISTENCE

Milfy Weeks and I decided to go fishing at Big Owl Lake south of the Troy community. The problem with going fishing in that lake was getting to it. We stopped at the road and put the boat in the creek. This particular time the water was way down, which meant there wasn't much water in the creek. We had to get out of the boat and drag it a lot of the way and every hundred feet or so there was a beaver dam that we had to pull the boat across. Each time we would try to decide if we were going to turn around and go back instead of crossing and going ahead. When we finally got to the lake, we were so tired and had spent so much time getting there we only had a few minutes to fish. But Milfy caught a huge bass, which made it all worthwhile. It was the only one caught before we started for the truck.

Our labors in Christ should be as persistent as the apostle Paul's were. He sums his efforts up in 2 Timothy 4:7-8: "I have fought a good fight, I have finished my course, I have kept the faith: Henceforth there is laid up for me a crown of righteousness, which the Lord, the righteous judge, shall give me at that day: and not to me only, but unto all them also that love his appearing."

Chapter 22

ALGOMA DOVE HUNT: BLACK AND BLUE – *DESIRE*

We had a dove field north of Algoma on my uncles' place where we farmed soybeans. We actually spent more time picking up roots on this particular field than we did farming it. I think if I could take my kids picking up roots a few times, then they would enjoy picking peas and working around the house. This particular year, we had worlds of doves. There was a small pond in the middle of the place and the doves were flocking to it. My brother, Barry, had a single shot H & R 20-gage. We counted twenty-five boxes of shells that he shot in one day. At the end of the day he would take a shot, it would knock him off the bucket, he would cry a little, and then get up and shoot again. He couldn't have been more than eleven or twelve years old. This was more than twenty years ago and I remember that we harvested a lot of doves, but I so vividly remember my brother's desire to shoot doves.

> The desire that he had is exemplary of the desire that we should have to learn more about and fellowship with our Savior. "But whoso looketh into the perfect law of liberty, and continueth therein, he being not a forgetful hearer, but a doer of the work, this man shall be blessed in his deed."
>
> —James 1:25

Chapter 23

SCUM FROG
BULL FROG –
PLAGUE

Scott Hatcher and I were bass fishing in a watershed lake somewhere and were having a pretty good morning fishing. The bass were hitting top-water baits, which is always the most fun time to fish. My favorite baits for top-water fishing were scum frogs and torpedoes. Torpedoes were the best in open water and scum frogs were great for fishing in the moss. Torpedoes had treble hooks and required you to set the hook immediately, which is natural. Scum frogs required you to wait a few seconds and let the fish get it well in his mouth. If you have ever tried this then you know that waiting is not natural, especially after the fish has boiled the water or even jumped out of the water after your lure. Instinct makes you set the hook immediately.

I was casting my scum frog up next to the bank from the boat and I had a small hit. A small hit can be confusing, because sometimes the bigger bass don't actually hit the bait; they just kind of suck it under the water. It hit again and close observation revealed that a bullfrog was trying to eat my lure. The frog finally got the bait in his mouth and I reeled him in. The bait was almost bigger than the frog's mouth!

I don't know if this frog was extra hungry or not, but think of the frogs that plagued Egypt when Moses was getting ready to lead the Israelites out. Exodus 8:6 says, "And Aaron stretched out his hand over the waters of Egypt; and the frogs came up, and covered the land of Egypt." I would imagine that frogs covering the land would eat anything they could get their mouth around. What a scary thought. No wonder Pharaoh gave in, albeit temporarily.

Chapter 24

TWO BIG FISH –
MISTAKES

When we were kids, my friend, David Tutor, and I went fishing behind our house at a neighbor's. We had to walk about half a mile through the woods to get to the ponds we wanted to fish. We fished a while with little success in the large pond; we were checking out what the fish were biting before we went to the small pond. It was fresh water spring fed and in the side of a wooded hill. The pond was very clear and we knew there was a huge bass in it, because we could see it every once in a while. In the large pond, we only caught a few small bass.

While at the big pond, I was having trouble with my reel. I threw a plastic worm way out into the middle and the line jammed up. I spent a few minutes trying to straighten out the mess on my spinning reel, then I reeled in the slack. When I tried to reel in my plastic worm, I thought it had sunk right onto a log, because I couldn't budge it. I was hung up. Then the log started to move away and I knew I had a big one. His side would shine each time he would get close while I was trying to reel him in. David got out into the water and helped get him on the bank. We fished a little while longer there and then went to the small pond.

When we got to the small pond, we immediately saw the big bass lurking around. He looked like a dark shadow almost two feet long. We threw everything in our tackle box at him to no avail. Then we went back to the plastic worm and tried it for a while. You could drag it right by his face and he would just watch it go by. Finally, I thought about the mess-up in the other pool and threw the worm out in front of him. I let it sink to the bottom out of sight. All of a sudden, the fish turned downward and started toward my worm. He went out of sight and then my line started to tighten up. I set the hook and the fight was on!

We walked home that afternoon by the highway instead of through the woods. One of my neighbors took my picture with the two fish. I put them in the freezer to keep until I could afford to get them mounted, but threw them away a few years later when we cleaned out the freezer.

Just like the mess-up with my reel, we make mistakes in life that do not turn out too badly. God can use our mistakes for many things—Romans 8:28—and one is to teach us. David sinned grievously with Bathsheba and then against her husband. Later, God blessed David and Bathsheba with a son, Solomon, a man of wisdom. The lineage runs all the way to Jesus.

Chapter 25

THE OLD DEER CAMP – *FAMILY*

When I first started deer hunting, we had an old shotgun house for a deer camp at Big Creek in Calhoun County. It had four or five rooms all in a row. I would go there with my Uncle Mike, and most of the people there were family on my mother's side. We had to draw water from a well to water the hounds and to wash dishes. Anyone who missed a deer was logged down as the next person to have to wash dishes. My cousins and I washed most of the dishes.

Some of my memories of the old deer camp are deer tenderloin meals, playing cards until late, listening to the rats burrow around in the walls, the driveway (you needed four-wheel drive to get up it), and cold outside meant cold inside. There was usually a pretty good argument sometime in the middle of the night about who had to get up and put wood in the stove.

My uncles always told that the rats were so big you couldn't catch them with a trap; you had to shoot them with a shotgun. There was a big rat hole going straight out of the wall into Uncle Floyd's mattress. One time they saw one sitting up on his hind legs in the hallway eating an onion. I never knew what to believe around there. I was just glad to be there.

As I think of my family and the joy I've had spending time with them, my Christian family comes to mind. "As we have therefore opportunity, let us do good unto all men, especially unto them who are of the household of faith."

—Galatians 6:10

Chapter 26

BIG FISH
AT LITTLE OWL –
WITNESSING

Scott Hatcher and I went bass fishing early one morning at Little Owl Lake in the Troy community. We fished hard for a while very unsuccessfully; we went through most everything that we normally use in our tackle boxes. Then we got down to the ones that we very rarely used. Scott was much more persistent than I was. I tied on a green and yellow minnow that was only supposed to go down two or three feet under water. It wasn't catching anything either. I fished with it for a while and did not want to tie anything else on my line. Scott was still changing lures. While he was doing so, I cast mine out as far as I could. I thought I would try to see how deep I could make it go so I jammed my rod down into the water, then I reeled as fast as I could reel. I then jammed my hand and arm down into the water even deeper and kept reeling. The big one almost jerked my rod out of my hand. After he spun the boat around a few times, we finally got him in. If you are going to catch fish, you have to go fishing. It is not always the one who is the best at fishing that catches them.

God told Simon Peter and Andrew that he would make them fishers of men. Our responsibility is to be a witness for Christ. "Go ye therefore and teach all nations, baptizing them in the name of the Father, and of the Son, and of the Holy Ghost:" Matthew 28:19. Too often, we worry about what we should say or how we should say something to help another person make the right decision about choosing Christ. Our responsibility is to tell them, not to convince them; the Holy Spirit will do that part.

Chapter 27

MUDCAT
AT ROYE LAKE –
RACISM

When my son was very small, he stayed at home with his mom, Jan, while I went fishing and camping with Allen Roye, J.D. Adams, and their oldest sons Adam, Seth, and Ben at Roye Lake. We caught a few fish, some of which were mudcats. The traditional catfish of the south is the channel cat, which is delicious. I had always heard that mudcats tasted like mud and were not very good to eat. Sitting around the campfire, I decided to cook one. I stuck a stick into a whole fish and held it over the fire until it was done. It tasted pretty good!

When Peter was directed in a vision to eat the unclean food, he wasn't sure what it meant. God told Peter in Acts 10:15, "What God hath cleansed, that call not thou common." Immediately afterward, the men showed up that God had directed Cornelious to send. God wanted Peter to share the Good News with the Gentiles. Aren't you glad that God doesn't exclude anyone from his love, mercy, and grace? We need only to accept them.

Chapter 28

ARMADILLO AIRPLANE - *CONFLICT*

I was hunting on the game area at Calhoun with my bow and arrows in a tall pine. I was between a large area of hardwoods to my left, a ten to fifteen-year-old pine thicket to my back, and a very thick mixed growth in front of me. I had seen a significant amount of buck sign in the hardwoods not far to my left. Early in the morning, I heard something out in front of me. It would rustle the leaves and pine needles for fifteen to twenty seconds coming toward me almost to where I could see it, and then turn back. Three or four times I came to full draw just waiting for the big buck to stick its head out from behind a tree. I hate to draw my bow before I know exactly what is out there. But once the deer gets so close to you, the conditions have to be perfect in order to get to draw on them. I just knew it had to be the buck that had made all the other sign making more right out in front of me. Finally an armadillo appeared about twenty yards out in front of me. I was frustrated to say the least. By this time I was about ready to go anyhow so I decided to test my shooting skills.

I exchanged the broad-headed arrow for an arrow with a field point. I didn't want to waste a good arrow on an armadillo. I drew back, aimed, and squeezed the release. The arrow flew true to its mark. It hit the armadillo directly in its armor broadside. The arrow was sticking halfway out on both sides. It took off down the hill running wide open like an airplane about to take off, then tripped and flipped over. It couldn't get back up; it could only move its feet and kick and look.

I started thinking about retrieving my arrow; I couldn't leave it with the armadillo. I climbed down out of the tree and eased up to him with him looking at me. I reached down and grabbed the fletching side of the arrow and yanked. When free, the armadillo instantly jumped straight up into the air and almost scared me to death. I am not sure which of us was trying to get away the fastest.

Sometimes things are not what they seem. One of the most important rules of hunting is to make sure of what you are shooting. No animal is worth taking a chance of shooting someone. When we deal with people, in church, at work, and at home, it is important that we know both sides of conflicts before we make rash decisions. Too many times, the obvious solution is not so obvious when you hear the other side of the story. "Seest thou a man that is hasty in his words? There is more hope of a fool than of him."

—Proverbs 29:20

Chapter 29

11-POINT –

HE MIGHT HAVE

SOMETHING BETTER

W e left for camp at Calhoun at 8:30 on Monday morning before Thanksgiving with plenty of clothes and a truckload of groceries. I spent most of the morning hunting while Chet tried out new hideouts in the middle of brushtops, then we moved to a cutover with very small pines. We didn't see very much deer sign so I was ready to leave. Chet didn't want to go; he wanted to walk to a clearing we could see far away.

We argued, but he took off so I followed. We began to follow some deer tracks down a logging road. We followed them a few hundred yards, then lost them. Chet was continually throwing sticks and rocks into the cutover on both sides of the road.

We went back to where we last saw the tracks and followed them into the cutover. The deer jumped up in front of us! I shot once as it went over the first ridge, twice as it went over the second, and twice as it went over the third. Then it stopped and looked at us and went on. I asked Chet if he saw the deer. He said he saw both of them. I only saw one so I thought it was possible I had hit one. We picked up our empty cartridges because Chet said he collected them, and then went to look for blood. By the time we got to where we last saw the deer, Chet claimed that I was pushing limbs into his face on purpose. The deer jumped up (he had been hit twice). We used all the rest of our shells on him, picked up our hulls, and went to check him out. We ate deer for supper, breakfast, lunch, and supper, and then Chet wanted it for breakfast the next morning.

I often wondered about the second deer that Chet saw. Bucks run together that time of year, so it is likely it was also a buck. Could it have been bigger than the first? Did it run over to the side and stop broadside allowing an easy shot? After this life, I will ask the One who knows. Don't you sometimes wonder if He will have time to answer silly questions like that?

> We should diligently seek God's plan because even when we think things are going good, he could have that bigger buck over on the side. "And Jabez called on the God of Israel saying, Oh that thou wouldest bless me indeed, and enlarge my coast, and that thine hand might be with me, and that thou wouldest keep me from evil, that it may not grieve me! And God granted him that which he requested."
>
> —1 Chronicles 4:10

Chapter 30

MUZZLELOADER DEER AT CALHOUN – *DETERMINATION*

I borrowed my Uncle Mike's muzzle loading rifle to go hunting at the game area in Calhoun County. It was a 45-caliber H&R. My cousin, Gary, and I were walking cutover to jump deer.

Walking cutover is an exciting way to hunt and most definitely a very challenging way as well. I heard him yelling and saw four or five deer about a hundred or hundred-and-fifty yards up the hill. They were moving really fast so I picked out a spot in front of them where I thought I might be able to see them. The first one came through and I located them. The second one came through and I was almost ready but not quite. The third one came through and I squeezed the trigger. Smoke went everywhere. When the smoke cleared, I thought I could see the deer on the ground, but there was too much cover to be sure. When we got to where the deer was, there was a lot of sign on the ground indicating the deer had been hit, but no deer. We began to trail the deer. We followed it for what seemed like hours and lost the trail.

The next day was Sunday. The game area doesn't allow Sunday hunting. This eliminated the temptation to skip church and go hunting that I sometimes struggled with. My girlfriend (soon to be my wife) and I went back on Sunday afternoon looking for the deer. The trail ended close to a beaver slough, which we thoroughly searched. We never found the deer!

Some people spend a significant part of their life looking for something to fill a void inside of them. In Ecclesiastes, Solomon describes this determined search as "vanity." Following are some of the things Solomon calls vain: striving for wisdom, great accomplishments, hard work, human religion, and wealth. The Bible says in Ecclesiastes 12:13-14, "Let us hear the conclusion of the whole matter: Fear God and keep his commandments: for this is the whole duty of man. For God shall bring every work into judgment, with every secret thing, whether it be good, or whether it be evil."

Chapter 31

ANTS IN PANTS AND YELLOWJACKETS – *GOSSIP*

Several times when dove hunting, I have managed to get tangled up with fire ants. It typically happens like this: I go out to a field and set up, looking to make sure that no one else is close by. I usually have a five-gallon bucket that I flip over to sit on. About the time I decide I know which way the first dove is going to come from, an annoying fire ant bites me on my leg or elbow. I look down to find they are all over me from about my waist down. I think at some point shortly after the first one stings, another ant gives the signal and they all start stinging me together. It is not at all uncommon for someone to strip down to their underwear to rid themselves of fire ants on a dove hunt. It is quite humorous to watch, but not very funny as a participant.

I once was cleaning out a lane to put a tree stand behind my house for deer hunting. I was using a chainsaw in very thick undergrowth. I vividly remember stepping into a semi-open spot and then looking around to decide the best direction to go next. While looking, something stung me on the leg. It hurt bad. I looked down and thought I saw something on me—my safety glasses had a little sweat in the bottom of them. Then yellowjackets (small yellow striped wasps) stung me fifty-two times all over! I dropped the chainsaw. I guess it ran out of gas because it was still running when I got out of hearing distance. I tore through the thicket like a madman. When I got to the house, Jan helped stop the bleeding on the top of my head and on the back of my legs. I went back a few days later and got my saw and destroyed the nest. It seems that a raccoon or something had dug up half of the nest, exposing it. I had stepped right in front of it. The vibration and noise of the saw had attracted them to me. I still don't know what gave them the signal to sting.

> The signal these awful creatures give to attack is similar to what happens at times in church. It seems that when someone gets down or has family or other problems, we don't always come to the rescue. Sometimes we gang up and use it as an opportunity to get a dig in that we wouldn't do if we weren't part the crowd. "As coals are to burning coals, and wood to fire: so is a contentious man to kindle strife."
> —Proverbs 26:21

Chapter 32

BOAT CAN –
MIND POLLUTION

We went fishing quite often at a lake near one of my uncles where we were required to tote or drag the boat a long way. We loved to fish there, because the bass were very healthy and someone usually caught a big one. Most of the time we carried my dad's ten-foot aluminum boat. It wasn't very heavy and it didn't hurt to drag it, or so we thought. We found out later that dragging it caused all the rivets to loosen up. We didn't think that deeply about it; we just wanted to go fishing. We carried a can with the boat that we used to bail water out. It got so bad that we spent a significant amount of time bailing water instead of fishing. We also argued about who had to bail. It sometimes got to where a good shift of weight would sink the boat.

When you think about the things that are available on the Internet and television to pollute our minds, it is easy to compare bailing with clearing out our minds. Bailing is not a bad thing. The bad thing is letting the water get in the boat or letting the filth enter our minds. Time spent bailing is time taken away from time doing something good. It is too easy to become complacent, because we are bombarded with so many bad things.

Chapter 33

COW TIPPIN AND SNAKE FISHIN – *SCARED*

We had always heard about cow tippin and decided to try it. Scott Hatcher and I drove up the road to a nearby pasture where we knew there were a lot of cows—and also a huge bull. Cow tippin is finding a cow that is sleeping standing up and running into it, knocking it down. I think it is kind of like snipe hunting; we were never successful at knocking one down. One particular time, we milled around the pasture and found a lot of cows but none asleep. The moon provided just enough light to see their outlines. All of a sudden Scott yelled and started running. I could hear the cows coming and looked around to see an entire stampede. I was so scared that I couldn't get leaned over fast enough. I think that I was running in place just like on the cartoons. When we finally got to safety, Scott let me know they weren't coming toward us—he just wanted to see if he could scare me.

Scott Hatcher, Mitch Montgomery, and I went fishing in a watershed lake that I don't remember a lot about. I do remember there was a creek running into it where we always caught a few fish. We took two boats. Scott and I were in the two-man water scamp and Mitch was in the eight-foot aluminum boat. We weren't catching many fish but we were seeing a lot of snakes. I think we either got into a nest or the snakes were breeding. They seemed to be everywhere on both sides of the creek just a few feet from the boat. As Mitch floated past us with no shirt on, I had an evil thought. The long red shad worm that I had tied on my line was rigged snagless, which meant the hook was not exposed. But it was long and wet. I flipped it right into the middle of Mitch's back. He came unglued and the race was on. We had a battery and trolling motor so he couldn't catch us.

> "But if ye forgive not men their trespasses, neither will your Father forgive your trespasses" Matthew 6:15. We could have held grudges for a long time but we didn't. We were good friends!

Chapter 34

GRANNY SHOT
THE HAWK –
TAKING CREDIT

My dad had been having trouble with hawks getting his chickens and small sheep and goats. We put a board up on a fence post at the barn with a steel trap on the top. The board was hinged to allow us to take it down and remove whatever got in it. The trap was a leg clamp type trap chained to the edge of the board but just sitting on top.

My grandma noticed a hawk on top of the pole one evening. She got her 38 snub nose revolver and started sneaking down to the barn. When she got within fifty to seventy-five yards, she took a shot at it and it fell off the pole. Within a short time my dad arrived and listened to the story of how she had shot the hawk. My brother arrived and an argument began. For those of you that don't know, that would be a miracle shot with a snub nose revolver.

Sometimes when people think they have accomplished something, it is better to leave them alone rather than tell them something different, especially if you are the only one who knows otherwise. I am not insinuating that we should say something that is not true, but too often we are more concerned about who gets the credit.

Chapter 35

TAKING THE KIDS
FISHING –
PRIORITIES

One of my friends let me know about a good lake to go bream fishing. The bream were bigger than your hand and on the bed. I got excited about it and loaded up the boat, seats, battery, trolling motor, fishing poles, tackle, crickets, paddles, and water cooler. My kids were four and seven years old. I hated to go do something on Saturday and not take them with me, so off we went. After a few minutes of fishing, it was clear the kids would rather play in the bucket of crickets, splash water on each other with the paddles, and drive the boat with the trolling motor. Even playing in the water cooler and slapping the water with the fishing poles was a lot better than fishing to them. Once my mind settled on the fact that we weren't going to wear the fish out, I had a much more enjoyable trip.

I think we often confuse our priorities. My priorities get mixed up when my kids go with me hunting or fishing. I easily forget how difficult it is for them to sit quiet and still. My desire to be successful has not changed. My definition of successful has changed. It seems successful to me if the kids have a desire to go back. It is more fun now to see them catch a fish or harvest game.

Chapter 36

SEINING THE POOL –
OBEDIENCE

We did some work on our fish pond when I was a little guy. Before we could work on the pond, we had to drain it down and seine it to get the fish out. We put several three-inch PVC pipes in to siphon the water over the levee. That was quite difficult to get started but ran problem free for several days. When we got the water down, we used a seine net to get the fish out. This required spreading a net out around the water and walking it through. It sounds simple but I was sinking three or four feet into the mud while trying to walk through. When we got the fish herded into a smaller area, they began jumping the net and trying to swim under. The weight of the fish also contributed to the trouble. We had a lot of help but not nearly enough. We had a fifty-five gallon drum full of one to three pound catfish to dress.

Seining a pond is kind of like mowing the grass to a kid. It looks like something you want to do until you actually get to do it. We obeyed my dad and helped, because that was the right thing to do. I asked my dad what he remembered about seining the pond. He said it was something he would never do again.

> I have tried to throw a net a few times with no success. I can imagine the work that Peter had done fishing all night when Jesus told them to cast their nets into the deep water. He had not caught a fish all night, but he obeyed what Jesus asked him to do and had to get another boat to hold all the fish that were in the net. Chapter 5 of Luke tells the story.

Chapter 37

SMOKEPOLE DEER – *CONCENTRATION*

My cousin, Gary, and I were walking cutover trying to jump out a deer one day hunting with our muzzleloaders. We eased off into the edge of a cutover. I was on the right and Gary was on the left with a hill kind of in between us. We got about halfway down the ridge and a deer jumped up to my right. It took a few steps and stopped to use the bathroom about sixty or seventy yards away. I raised my gun to my shoulder and thought, "Oh what a gravy shot." I aimed and fired. Instantly smoke filled the air from my black powder rifle. A few seconds later when the smoke cleared out enough for me to see, the deer was still in position. I didn't even scare it enough to ruin its bathroom break! I then proceeded to reload my rifle, which requires using a hammer to knock the base plug back up into the barrel. It won't close until you have completed this step. It then has to be loaded from the muzzle end. By the time I got all of this done the deer had finished up and moseyed off. I tell you this deer was concentrating on the task at hand.

> We are to concentrate on the mission that God has given us. "Peace I leave with you, my peace I give unto you: not as the world giveth, give I unto you. Let not your heart be troubled, neither let it be afraid."
>
> —John 14:27

Chapter 38

MULES AND HORSES – SPIRIT

We had a horse named Bones. He was bone skinny when we got him and rather easy to catch. As he began to fatten up, we realized that he was a very spirited horse. I hemmed him up one day in the barn trying to catch him to ride him. He kicked at me and hit a pole that supported the roof. His shoe print in the pole was a little higher than my chest. It is not much fun to see the bottom of a horse's foot.

We had a mule that we wanted to take hunting. We had to prove first that we could shoot off of him. My friend, David, and I talked my little brother, Barry, into doing the experiment for us. David and I usually teamed up against Barry in whatever we did such as boxing, wrestling, or football, so this was nothing unusual. We got the mule saddled up and took him out to where the grass was deep in order to have a soft landing. Barry used a 22 revolver with one bullet just like Barney Fife. We didn't want anything to happen with the pistol after the first shot. David and I propped on the fence in the barn fully expecting to see a good show. When Barry fired the pistol, the mule bolted straight out from under him. He looked like Wile E. Coyote when he steps off a cliff. It was like he was just sitting in the air before he crashed straight down to the ground.

> When we think of a spirited horse or mule, we think of them as very being active. The Holy Spirit living in us as Christians should make us active also. "But if the Spirit of him that raised up Jesus from the dead dwell in you, he that raised up Christ from the dead shall also quicken your mortal bodies by his Spirit that dwelled in you."
>
> —Romans 8:11

Chapter 39

FIRST DEER – HUMILITY

The first deer that I ever killed had been crippled and was trapped in a creek and could not get out. It was a doe that someone else had shot. At the time it was illegal to shoot a doe, but putting it out of its misery was the right thing to do. We handed the deer over to the game warden or compliance officer. It was a sad but relatively uneventful story. The bigger story is the number of years that I hunted without harvesting a deer. I would sometimes see fifteen or twenty deer in a day, but no bucks. I prayed regularly for God to let me harvest a deer. At the time I thought it must not have been important enough to God to spend his time working on. However, I think things that are important to us are also important to God. There was another reason, which I will find out for sure when I have eternity to spend with the Master. It could have been he wanted to instill a desire for hunting in me that would last a lifetime. Sometimes not getting what we want makes us want it that much more. And I truly believe that hunting and fishing are activities that keep a person from getting into trouble. It could have been that God wanted to control my pride or keep me humble. He knew what my mind and heart needed at that time.

> Peter was taught humility when Jesus washed his feet (John 13).1 Peter 5:6 says, "Humble yourselves therefore under the mighty hand of God, so that He may exalt you in due time."

Chapter 40

FISHING AT NOXUBEE – *SHIPWRECK*

Lee Spencer and I went fishing one day at Bluff Lake on the Noxubee Wildlife Refuge. A few days before we had spent an afternoon throwing rocks off the levy at a large tractor tire floating out in the lake (we realized it was the famous thirteen-foot alligator before it swam off). Back to fishing!

We used my dad's ten-foot flat-bottom aluminum boat. We put the boat in the water on the headquarters side of the lake and fished through the trees. When walking through the shallow water, we pulled the boat using a rope tied around our waist. The water was shallow enough that the boat wouldn't float while we were in it. Something made a huge splash a few feet from us. We both jumped back in the boat and watched a three-foot alligator swim away. We fished that spot long and hard with our boat sitting on the ground in ankle deep water before we decided to venture back out. We caught several bass on top-water baits and plastic worms.

When it started to get dark, we headed back for the truck. We worked our way through the small one to three-inch diameter saplings in about four-foot deep water. Lee was standing up in the front of the boat grabbing trees and pulling us along, while I was in the back using a paddle. Suddenly, Lee realized that he had grabbed a sapling with a four to five-inch diameter red wasp nest in the top of it. He got off balance and fell out of the boat. As he was going over, I compensated too much and flipped the boat. I found out later that the large alligator was on his mind just as it was mine. I think we probably set a record time for up righting a boat, throwing our stuff back in it, and getting ourselves back in.

> Acts 28 tells of the shipwreck that Paul was in while on his way to Rome as a prisoner. God protected him through the shipwreck and poisonous snakebite on the island of Malta. He still had a plan for Paul. God has a plan for each of us; He can handle anything, no matter the situation.

Chapter 41

SLINGING CHITLINS - CLEAN

My dad raised a couple of hogs and decided that January 1st would be a good day to kill them. It was a family affair. Some of our kin brought a couple of more hogs to my Granny's barn.

We began by starting the fires to get the big pots of water boiling. We used the hot water to scald the hair, so we could scrape it off the hogs. Someone brought a sausage grinder. Some of us were cutting up bacon, tenderloin, and getting hams ready to cure, while others were making the sausage and cooking out cracklins. My Aunt Hazel and I worked on the chitlins. Chitlins are the intestines of a pig. We cut them into foot long sections and squeezed the insides out of them like toothpaste through a tube. We then used hot water to clean them out. We would hold one end, fill the section with hot water, pinch the other end, and then slosh the water around. We did this several times until they were clean. Aunt Hazel cleaned them some more and cooked them a couple of weeks later. They were tasty but a couple of weeks are not quite enough time in between cleaning and cooking. At one time while we were working, my Granny said she had called Uncle Paul and he was going to come and get the lungs, livers, and heads. We thought it was funny when my cousin Rolo immediately said we need to have some kind of benefit for Uncle Paul.

> The stuff that we were slinging out of those chitlins was foul and nasty. It could be compared to sin or something evil. "Wash you, make you clean; put away the evil of your doings from before mine eyes; cease to do evil."
>
> —Isaiah 1:16

Chapter 42

BIG BASS
LITTLE HOOK –
FAITHFUL

For a while at my Granny's fishpond, the best way to catch a big bass was to start out with a small bream hook. We baited it with a mealworm or a cricket, then flipped it out five or ten feet from the bank and waited. Usually within a few minutes a bream would bite the hook. Then we would take our time dragging it in because lurking nearby were several four to six-pound bass. The water was very clear so we could see all the action. The bass would attack the little bream that was already on the hook. Sometimes it would spit the bream out and sometimes we would get the fish to the bank. We were using small tackle also, which makes the fight a lot more fun.

Matthew 25 gives us the parable of the talents. Sometimes what we are fishing with isn't as important as trying to do what God instructs us to do. In the parable of the talents, the man had used his five talents to gain five more. His Lord said unto him, "Well done, thou good and faithful servant: thou hast been faithful over a few things, I will make thee ruler over many things: enter thou into the joy of thy lord."

—Matthew 25:21

Chapter 43

TURTLE REFLEXES

Papa Higgins took us fishing one time, but I don't remember where. The only thing I remember about the fishing trip was catching a turtle. I was using a cane pole, line, cork, and hook. When I got the turtle to the bank, Papa took the turtle and pulled its head out of the shell and cut it off. He had to do that to get the hook out of its mouth. I believe that he asked me if I thought the turtle was dead and I said, "Sure, its head is gone." He flipped the turtle over on its back and dropped it in an anthill. Within seconds the turtle's legs came out of the shell and it began to kick ferociously. The ants were stinging the turtle and its reflexes were still strong enough to try to get him away from the danger.

Unlike the turtle, Cain had a choice in his reaction when God did not accept his gift. Genesis 4 tells the story. We have a choice concerning our reaction in almost every situation. The world tells us "I couldn't help it" or "I was born that way" or "I didn't know any better" or "I didn't think about it" or "It wasn't born yet." Unlike the turtle, we still have a head. When we sin we will suffer the consequences even if we are Christians.

Chapter 44

ALGOMA 6-POINT –

COURAGE

My brother Barry, Tommy Duke, and I went rabbit hunting at Algoma. There was a place we liked to hunt close to my Granddaddy Crawford's place. We had our two old beagles, Sissy and Fluffy, and eight or nine young dogs. The dogs jumped something out in front of us about a hundred yards and out of sight. A few seconds later, Sissy and Fluffy showed up right next to us. One of us made the comment: "Well it's not a rabbit." Tommy took off running, trying to get in front of the puppies. Barry and I walked ahead and out into a sage grass field.

We could hear the dogs clearly across the creek in the woods on the other side. Boom boom boom boom boom—five shots rang out in the direction where Tommy had gone. Seconds later a deer jumped the creek and came out into the sage grass field in a full sprint. Barry and I were out in the middle the field. The deer was several hundred yards from us sprinting from our left to our right. The deer did not run in a normal lope. It was stretched out low to the ground and looked like an airplane going down the runway to take off. We got ready but really didn't think the deer would make it to us before going into the woods. Suddenly it turned and headed directly toward us. Barry and I were only ten yards apart. I was dressed in fluorescent orange and thinking there was no way it would keep coming toward us. But it came directly toward me! When it got within about fifteen or twenty yards, Barry and I began shooting. The deer veered off his direct path toward me, but instead of going away he veered in between us. I vividly remember my brother and myself raising our guns as we swung through with the deer. We never pointed at each other. The deer was struggling as he went past us but he made it through without us knocking him down after ten shots at close range. We caught the dogs and then blood trailed him for a few hundred yards. We met a friend on the highway that had a Bluetick Hound. He turned the dog on the trail of the buck. The dog later came out chasing a doe.

When I think of the deer's point of view and the decisions he made, I think of Peter and his time in prison. Once the deer got so close to us, he was better off going ahead than stopping and turning around. The deer was definitely in a time of trouble and fear. In Acts 12, Peter had the kind of courageous attitude that we should have when faced with fear. "The Lord is my light and my salvation; whom shall I fear? The Lord is the strength of my life; of whom shall I be afraid?"

—Psalm 27:1

Chapter 45

CLIFF JUMPING – *ABSTAIN*

One of our favorite things to do is go camping at Lewis Smith Lake in Alabama. We have gone a few times each summer for as long as I can remember. My wife and kids like it as well. My kids told me what they like about Smith Lake: skiing, the smell of the lake, jumping off cliffs, the cabin, riding the boat, swimming, riding the tube, and turtle rock. I think my favorite thing about Smith Lake is the smooth water. In the mornings and late in the evening, the water is as smooth as glass. It is like looking in a mirror when you lean over while skiing.

We have always enjoyed jumping off the rocks. The first thing we must do when jumping off a cliff or rock is to check the depth of the water. The easy way is to use a depth finder. There are drop offs as deep as fifty to seventy-five feet under the water. Most of the time we don't have a depth finder, so we tie something heavy to a ski rope, or someone swims straight down to check the depth. Swimming straight down under the water into the unknown can be quite unnerving. There are tales of catfish big enough to swallow a person whole. I usually have my eyes shut so I am feeling for the bottom or feeling for rocks. If you aren't careful you can swim into underwater rocks or bushes. You can also swim up into crevices under the water if you are going straight down the wall. You can tell that I prefer to drop the end of a ski rope to check the depth.

> Testing the water can be compared to flirting with sin. It is sometimes easy to think: "It won't ever get out of hand!" The Bible says, "Abstain from all appearance of evil."
>
> —1 Thessalonians 5:22

Chapter 46

PICKING UP CHUNKS –

LABOR

One of my least favorite things to do was always picking up roots. My dad and uncle farmed soybeans. They always seemed to trade for land that had to be cleaned up. I am sure it was not as bad as it seemed when I was a kid, but I hated picking up roots. My cousins and I would walk around the field picking up chunks and throwing them in the back of a pickup or bean truck. Each time the field was disked over, there was a whole new set of roots on top of the ground to be picked up. My brother got out of it quite a bit, because he had baseball practice. We always tried to come up with a way to make him pay for missing all the work, but our attitude was unjustified.

I think Christ is speaking more of our mental anguish in Matthew chapter 11:28-30, "Come unto me all ye that labour and are heavy laden and I will give you rest. Take my yoke upon you and learn of me for I am meek and lowly in heart: and ye shall find rest in your souls. For my yoke is easy, and my burden is light." God invites us to him and then promises to give us peace of mind when we submit our lives to his will.

Chapter 47

MOUSE BITE – GIANT

When I was a kid, I was disking a field in Algoma getting it ready to plant, driving a 9700 Ford tractor with a cab on it. If you went around the field until the part that was not disked was all in the middle, then the small game would always come running out across the clean cut dirt ground. I had caught small rabbits before, but on this particular day a mouse came out. I stopped the tractor and got out to catch it. I stepped on it and reached down to pick it up. It looked like a dog snarling its lips up to growl! It bit and punched a hole in my index finger. I grabbed my finger and started jumping around. The mouse ran away. I was angry and tried to catch it again with no success.

One of my favorite stories in the Bible is about David and Goliath. That mouse probably thought of me as a giant and was successful just as David was. I am not sure that God was on the mouse's side like he was David's. God might have been letting me know I was supposed to be on the tractor working.

> I Samuel chapter 17: 50-31 says, "So David prevailed over the Philistine with a sling and with a stone, and smote the Philistine, and slew him; but there was no sword in the hand of David. Therefore David ran, and stood upon the Philistine, and took his sword, and drew it out of the sheath thereof, and slew him, and cut off his head therewith. And when the Philistines saw their champion was dead, they fled."

Chapter 48

WALL HANGER – *REFUGE*

We had a few ponds close to our trailer in Starkville when I was attending Mississippi State University. One was down the road about a mile or so. One day, I loaded my fishing stuff in my AMC four-door Concord. I facetiously called it a chick magnet. It was brown where the paint hadn't come off. I remember once four of us got into the Tupelo Fair and Carnival free when they waved us around to the employee parking. We didn't know what was going on, but they must have thought we were fair workers in the Concord. However, the Concord was a fine hunting and fishing vehicle.

I drove to the lake about a mile down the road and went bass fishing. I had been seen a large bass on the levee, but had not been able to catch him. I cast a couple of times going toward where I last saw him using a black with white stripes tiny torpedo top-water lure. There was a dead tree hanging out over the water marking the spot. I cast the torpedo right up next to the bank under the dead tree. I didn't even twitch it; I just let it set there. It looked like a bream hit it, because it just barely bobbled and then went under. I set the hook and the fight was on! The fish came up one time and tried to throw the hook. He jumped and shook. I saw that the treble hook of the torpedo was hooked in the skin on the outside of the fish's lip. It was hanging by a thread. I tried to hold as little tension as I could on the line to get him in. This was the biggest fish I had ever caught. When I got him to the bank, I grabbed my other stuff and we ran to the car. I dropped him on the floor and headed home. We found someone at the University with a set of scales and weighed him in at 7.25 pounds. He is on my wall today.

> There is a place to turn when life is hanging by a thread and you are trying to keep the tension to a minimum. "The Lord also will be a refuge for the oppressed, a refuge in times of trouble."
>
> —Psalm 9:9

Chapter 49

FISHING ON PARK LANE – LUKEWARM

There were three ponds within walking distance of our trailer at Mississippi State. When the weather was nice, we fished them often. David Tutor and I were trying to catch bass one year when they were on the bed. There were two or three large bass that swirled the water around their bed but wouldn't bite a lure. David went and got a bucket of minnows and we made a plan. We sneaked up the back of the levee where we could see the fish. He flipped a minnow over into the bed. The bass swam around the minnow a few times and then went up close to it looking at it—within an inch or two. The bass then opened its mouth and sucked the minnow into it. She then spit it right back out. She did this three or four times before leaving the area. David was going to try snatching the hook when the minnow was in the fish's mouth but she didn't do it anymore. A few days later we caught several big bass on the bed with a purple worm.

> "I know thy works, that thou art neither cold nor hot: I would thou wert cold or hot. So then because thou art lukewarm, and neither cold nor hot, I will spue thee out of my mouth"
>
> —Revelation 3:15-16

Chapter 50

GREEN HEAD
MALLARD PHEASANT –
GUIDANCE

Several of us went pheasant hunting in Iowa. Our home office had closed a plant there and moved the production to our plant. We made friends with some of the folks there and they set us up pheasant hunting. We started walking in the first field we were sent. The ground was very dark almost like Skuna bottom mud. When I stepped on it, I was pleasantly surprised that the mud didn't stick to my feet. If I had made the same walk in Skuna bottom, I would have come out the other side with fifteen pounds of mud on each foot. We had my dad's bird dog and another dog. They were hunting along beside us and flushed the first bird. When it flew up, I saw the green head and immediately refrained from shooting it, because it was a brilliant green just like a Mallard duck. Someone else shot at it and knocked it down. It immediately hit the ground running and ran probably half a mile before it went out of sight. After taking a good ragging for thinking the pheasant was a duck, I did better the rest if the trip. It was the first pheasant I had ever seen!

In life things aren't always as they appear. God knows what is real. He also has a plan for each of us. "In all thy ways acknowledge him, and he shall direct thy paths."

—Proverbs 3:6

Chapter 51

HOMEMADE BACKPEDALING CRAWFISH –
WAIT AND LOSE

We did a lot of fishing at my Uncle George's pond for a while. The pond was spring fed and clear and the fish were all very healthy. When cleaning the fish we noticed that a lot of them had crawfish in their stomachs, but I couldn't find an artificial one to use as bait. I decided to make one. I made the prototype out of wood and used lead to weight it for the action that I wanted. Crawfish use their tail to move backwards along the bottom in very quick motions. When I first took my new plug fishing, I cast it twice with no success. I then threw it up close to the bank and hit a log breaking the tail off of it. I threw it back in the tackle box to work on at a later date. Six months later I saw a thirty-minute infomercial on TV for an artificial crawfish. I had waited and missed a good opportunity.

Sometimes it is considerably easier to wait before witnessing to someone, or not to witness at all. We could miss a blessing, and they miss hearing about Christ. "Therefore I say unto you, Take no thought for your life what ye shall eat, or what ye shall drink; nor yet for your body, what ye shall put on. Is not the life more than meat, and the body than raiment?"

—Matthew 6:25

Chapter 52

THORNS AND THISTLES - WORK

When we were little my Granddaddy Westmoreland paid us to hoe thistles in the pasture and catch perch out of the pool. He would pay us a penny each to catch the pond perch out of the pool. I am not sure if he didn't want the perch in the pool or he just wanted a reason to pay us something. He also sometimes paid us to hoe the thistles or briar weeds in the pasture. I am sure that this was legitimate work. I think he paid us as much as a nickel each to hoe the thistles sometimes. It was pretty hard work for a little guy. Catching perch was fun. My Granny and Granddaddy ran the County Old Folks Home. We tried to catch enough perch to get a drink and a snack out of the machines at the County Home. We had to catch forty-five fish to get a coke and a snack. We spent a lot of time in the County Home. We grew to love many of the old folks there. That is where I learned to play and enjoy checkers.

> After the sin of Adam and Eve in the garden, God made the rule that men have to work. "Thorns also and thistles shall it bring forth to thee; and thou shalt eat the herb of the field."
>
> —Genesis 3:18

Chapter 53

BAREFOOT SKIING – PRIDE

Scott Hatcher and I considered ourselves to be somewhat better than a lot of folks at a lot of things, but we were put in our place trying to ski barefooted. We didn't have any of the equipment that makes bare footing easier. We just tried it behind his bass boat, and started out skiing on a slalom. We found some smooth water and sped the boat up as fast as it would go. I pulled my left foot out of the back slot on the ski. I moved it around beside my right foot and put it down into the water. I then began to ease my weight to my left foot. When I thought I was basically skiing on one bare foot, I began to raise my right foot and the ski up out of the water to release it. I think I got the ski up, but couldn't get it off my foot. Then the crash began. I think I was going too fast to actually fall into the water.

I just skimmed along the top doing summersaults like the snow skiing commercial for the "agony of defeat," Looking back, I can't believe I even tried it, but what's worse I tried it again. And, yes, Hatch tried it too. If you ever think you want to try barefoot skiing the way we did, you can get the same effect by getting a boat up to top speed and jumping out the side.

> "Pride goeth before destruction, and a haughty spirit before a fall."
>
> —Proverbs 16:18

Chapter 54

FIRST BOW SHOT –
CHANGE OF MIND

When I first started hunting with a bow and arrow, I had a bow that would only pull about forty-five to fifty pounds. Someone put it in perspective for me once: "Are you still hunting with that old 'Indian'?" I used it when I was in college. My roommate and I got where we could hit a dot in the center of a paper plate on a hay bale consistently at thirty-five to forty yards. The secret was knowing the yardage. It had so much drop that if you misjudged the distance by five yards, you would almost surely miss the plate.

I was hunting on the Noxubee refuge one afternoon just walking along looking for deer. I walked through some Palmetto bushes into some honeysuckle and a deer appeared. It was broadside about twenty yards from me, or so I judged. I raised the bow, drew, put the pin across its heart, and released. The arrow flew straight but missed just below the deer's chest. The deer took five or six steps forward, and then stopped to look where the arrow had hit the honeysuckle, so it was facing away from me. I mentally noted twenty-five yards, grabbed another arrow, knocked it, raised my bow, and came to full draw. I hesitated. Now I was fully confident this shot would find its target! How many times do you get two chances with the deer broadside at twenty-five steps? Closer examination of the deer revealed that it still had spots. They were faded out but definitely still there. I decided not to shoot.

> God did something different several times in the Bible based on the petition of different people. He listened to the pleading of Abraham for Lot in Genesis chapter 18. He listened to the pleading of Moses for the Israelites in Numbers chapter 14. Of course, God knows what is going to happen and who is going to do what, and even who is going to accept him. We were put here to please him and I sometimes wonder if he just chooses not to look that far ahead. "The effectual fervent prayer of a righteous man availeth much"
>
> —James 5:16

Chapter 55

QUAIL HUNTING –

ENVY

When I first got big enough to go hunting, my dad took me quail hunting. It was his passion. I often wonder why God gave him such a passion for one outdoor sport and gave me a love for almost all of them in no particular order. The first gun I used was a double barrel 20-gage that had once belonged to my great granddad on my dad's side. Daddy had refinished the gun including the metal, stock, and forearm. He had also repaired some internal problems.

The dog pointed and we walked into a covey of birds. The flush of a covey of quail is about as exciting as hunting gets. The flutter is deafening as they boil off the ground going in every direction. I took a shot into the covey. A covey shot seems like a good thing to do, but is usually fruitless. You must first pick out a bird, focus, and shoot. When I took the gun down, I set it to the ground (it was very heavy for me). As it hit the ground, the other barrel went off just in front of my face. I remember being terribly unnerved and frightened..

A couple of years later, Daddy and I were hunting on my uncle's one hundred acres at Algoma and scattered a covey of quail. When the covey scatters, the birds spread out and fly a few hundred yards and set back down. We were walking along a field road and a bird got up right in front of us. In my mind I can see the bird flying like it was in slow motion directly away from us. As I sometimes did because quail hunting involved a lot of walking, I had my gun across my shoulders behind my head like a weightlifting bar. I knew my dad was quick to the shot on quail. That didn't stop me from giving my best effort to get the first shot. In my rush to raise the gun off my shoulders, I rammed it into the back of my head almost giving myself a concussion. Daddy got that one. I regularly beat him to the shot and then usually he killed the bird.

> Teaching and fellowshipping ministries should aim for the congregation, but individual attention is also necessary. I don't think my desire to beat my dad to the kill was considered envy as much as it was a desire to confirm that I was getting better. In some cases it could have been envy. God tells us about envy. "A sound heart is the life of the flesh: but envy the rottenness of the bones."
>
> —Proverbs 14:30

Chapter 56

BINGO AND THE LITTLE HORSES — *HATRED*

My uncle brought us a newborn deer that he had found while clipping grass. We named it Bingo and put it in a barn stall with a newborn goat (Fred) so that it could nurse on Fred's mama. The mama goat didn't like it too much, but she let Bingo nurse while Fred was nursing. Daddy's miniature horses and Bingo didn't get along, but Bingo was always fast enough to get away from them. She would either go through or over the fence. I don't know why the horses hated Bingo. I once tried to outrun Bingo on the four-wheeler (a Honda 300). She sped up each time I went up a gear. When I ran out of gears, she ran off and left me. She would disappear for a couple of days at a time but always came back. We tried to put her up during hunting season. By the way, Fred the goat was a female. I never noticed until she was expecting kids of her own.

My dad and I were hanging up a deer that I had shot behind Granny's when we heard the beagles bumping around down below the fish pond. I jumped in the truck and went around on the highway to catch the dogs, just in case they came out in the road. A minute later, I heard a shot at the barn. I went back to the barn and Daddy had killed a doe. He said the dogs never came out, but two horses came out chasing three deer. Two of the deer jumped the fence between my Granny's house and her log cabin. The horses chased the other deer around between the barn and the pool where my dad killed it.

> The miniature horses may have started hating deer when Bingo was very small. She was poor, helpless, and alone. The Bible tells us about hating the underdog: "The poor is hated even of his own neighbor: but the rich hath many friends. He that despiseth his neighbor sinneth: but he that hath mercy on the poor, happy is he."
>
> —Proverbs 14:20-21

Chapter 57

SISSY AND FLUFFY – TRUSTWORTHY

My friend and I bought a couple of beagles when we were in high school to take rabbit hunting. They were very young but already running rabbits. Sissy was the jump dog and by far everyone's favorite. She was a hot nosed dog, meaning that when she barked there was something close by that either just moved around or was about to. Fluffy was cold nosed, meaning whatever she was barking at might have passed by yesterday. When Sissy barked people listened. She was trustworthy like a person who tells the truth. Their barks were very distinguished. Sissy barked with a high pitched squeal, while fluffy had a long drawn out deep howl. They sounded really good together.

Once we were hunting and lost the dogs. It sounded like they went out of hearing distance very quickly. As we went toward them, they sounded like they were far away but were changing directions very quickly. We didn't walk very far until they sounded like they were behind us. Going back and forth a couple of times we found they had run into a hole. A little while later they came out dragging a possum they had chased into that same hole.

I called Sissy our jump dog earlier. This is because she hunted harder than anyone else and usually jumped the rabbit. The most valuable dog to a rabbit hunter who wants to kill rabbits is the jump dog. There is almost always one dog that does most of the work before the rabbit is on the run. This happens because the other dogs know that if they mosey around long enough, the jump dog will get up a rabbit. Does this remind you of anything in your Christian walk?

If you kept a close eye on Sissy, you could tell when she was about to jump a rabbit. She would get excited, her tail would start wagging, and most of the time she would lunge in the direction where she thought the rabbit went. Sometimes you would hear the distinct squeal of the rabbit as she caught it in the bed. She was always so proud of herself when she caught one. The most interesting time to watch her was when she lunged toward the rabbit before she started barking. It was almost like she didn't want to bark because she knew she was more likely to catch it if she didn't bark. The bark would swell up inside her like she would almost burst, and then she would begin squealing like she was singing a tune.

When Sissy got older, she wasn't as able to keep up with her children and grandchildren. The week between Christmas and New Year we hunted them pretty hard for a few days in a row. After a couple of days, it would take Sissy a few minutes to be able to walk around when we got home from hunting. Each day we decided we wouldn't take her hunting the following day. But the next morning she was jumping on the fence wanting to go just like the rest of them. We could only hunt a precious few days of the year, so seemed a shame to leave her in the pen when everyone else was going hunting. She talked us into it. That was her last year. She died in the night but thoroughly enjoyed her last season in the field. If it is possible for a dog to have a mission, I think Sissy completed hers.

> When God puts someone specific on your heart to tell about him, the urge to do so swells up inside until your nervousness or hesitation is overcome by your sense of what is right. When Samuel heard God call him as a young boy, I suspect that there was no trouble hearing. There was only trouble understanding. If we are not expecting God to speak to us then we may not recognize his voice when he does. Where do you stand in your mission? Paul said in 2 Timothy 4:7, "I have fought a good fight, I have finished my course, and I have kept the faith:"

Chapter 58

BEAR THE DOG –
THE LORD
KNOWS BEST

My dad always raised quail to train his bird dogs. He had a pen at my Granddaddy Crawford's house on one end of the barn. We always had trouble with animals getting into the pen and killing the birds. Raccoons, foxes, possums, skunk, and snakes were the usual culprits. He put an electric fence around the bottom of the wall about one to two inches off the ground. We had a Feist dog named Bear who was always mean to everyone who came near her. She weighed about five pounds, but her demeanor made her seem about fifty pounds! She was especially mean when she got older and the black fur turned to gray.

We were out at the barn one day when Bear got into the electric fence. She rolled around on it and couldn't get away. I reached down and grabbed her and pulled her off the fence. In the commotion, she bit through my hand between my thumb and index finger. She thought I was the one shocking her!

Every time anyone told an electric fence story, one of my uncles had to tell about the time he was urinating off the tractor onto an electric fence. It must have been an interesting sight to see. I think that probably most folks are not aware that urine is an excellent conductor of electricity.

When I think about the dog and her accusatory bite it reminds me of the human thought process when things aren't going our way. In some situations, I can't correlate how things work together for good for those who love God. I believe what Isaiah said that the Lord said: "For as the heavens are higher than the earth, so are my ways higher than your ways, and my thoughts than your thoughts" Isaiah 55:9. The Lord knows how and he will make it all work out in the end.

Chapter 59

TRUCK STUCK –
COMMUNICATION

Somewhere around 1990 or 1991, we decided to go mud riding on the Jackson Lake road. I had an '82 Chevy four-wheel drive pickup. I don't remember exactly how we all got into the truck, but it was the night that I officially met my future wife. That evening she had been a bridesmaid in one of her friend's wedding. Mitch, Gina, JJ, Jan and I went mud riding—five grown folks on the bench seat of my truck. It was a fairly uneventful mud ride except that I got the truck stuck in a big mud hole right on top of the levee miles from anywhere. I have a mental picture of my wife in the parking lot of Pontotoc High School where we loaded into the truck and another in the headlights of the stuck truck. She was (and is) beautiful! I don't think I could have made a worse first impression, but at least she knew the real me from the very beginning. We didn't have cell phones but we had a CB radio just like the eighteen-wheeler drivers use. After exhausting the other means of getting the truck out, We tried the CB. JJ knew someone with a base station in her house. We called her on the CB and got her to call Scott Hatcher to come pull us out. He arrived with a grin on his face.

Being able to effectively communicate got us through a time of need. "Pray without ceasing" 1 Thessalonians 5:17. If we communicate with the master, He can help us in all tough times.

Chapter 60

RABBIT HUNTING THE WATERWAY – *ALMIGHTY*

A few years ago, we loaded up the boat and went rabbit hunting on the Tombigbee Waterway. There was an island there that had swamp and hillbilly rabbits. It was probably a mile or two long surrounded by the old river on one side and the new river on the other. Carrying boys and dogs in a fourteen-foot aluminum boat makes for a very interesting ride.

We parked the boat and tied off to a tree on the upstream end of the island. There must have been a smorgasbord of food there on the island, because we always saw several deer and rabbits. The dogs jumped a herd of deer that crossed the old river on the south side. It was a good place to take young beagles because the dogs usually didn't want to swim the river if they happened to jump a deer. I think we killed a few rabbits, but the most interesting thing happened when we got back to where the boat was supposed to be. It wasn't there! We thought we were sure about the exact spot where we left it—we even found the tree it was tied to—but it just wasn't there.

We walked a little piece to where we could see down river and saw the boat a few hundred yards away about fifteen to twenty feet off the bank. Whew! We brainstormed through a few ideas about how to get the boat to the bank. We didn't come up with any very good ones and had about decided that someone was going to have to swim for it when we saw a barge coming. A barge is a huge boat that is strictly for transporting materials from one place to another. They displace an enormous amount of water. Each container is probably seventy-five to one-hundred feet wide and about one-hundred-and-fifty feet long. They line up several in a row and push or pull them with a smaller boat. When the barge passed by, the five to six-foot waves pushed the boat right to us.

Several questions came to mind when this happened: 1) Who tied the boat? 2) What kind of knot did they use? 3) Will they ever tie it that way again—I don't think so!

We went through a range of emotions such as: Fear: We have lost the boat. How do we get home? Elation: there's the boat! I can't believe we found it. Helplessness: our means of transportation is there. But how do we use it? Thankfulness: the barge brought it right to us!

Almighty God can take care of the fear and helplessness. He is bigger than the barge! He provided us a boat to reach eternal life in Jesus. There is no work that we can do in this life to provide for our own salvation. We must only accept the free gift that is offered to us. In Luke 17, Jesus healed ten lepers. One of them immediately returned to praise and thank him. "And he said unto him, Arise, go thy way: thy faith hath made thee whole."

—Luke 17:19

Chapter 61

SNOW CREAM FOR SUPPER AND BREAKFAST – *WHATEVER IT TAKES*

For a while we had a trailer for a deer camp within a mile of the headquarters of the Game Management area in Calhoun County. We hunted one day in a good snow, which is three or four inches in Mississippi. We decided to stay the night in camp, because we had some dogs still out. I had a few puppies that were half beagle and half bird dog. They were excellent deer dogs, because we could keep up with them but they hunted like bird dogs. They covered a lot of ground using their nose to wind the deer instead of sniffing the trails. One particular one I didn't want to leave in the snow all night was named Foot. She was named Foot, because her foot had swelled up like a balloon for some reason while she was a baby. She was lemon and white and looked just like a miniature pointer bird dog.

We made some snow cream for supper. We mixed milk and sugar with a little vanilla and quickly added the snow. It is better than homemade ice cream! After supper, we stuffed the pan out under the trailer for breakfast the next morning. We made a late night search and found our missing dogs. My Uncle Cecil Higgins, Gary Higgins, and I were the only three staying that night. The only heat we had in the trailer came from the stove, so we left it on all night. It was so cold, I remember being sore from the weight of all the blankets that I had on my bed.

The next morning we had a good laugh. Uncle Cecil had used some garbage bags to stuff in a hole in the wall. He had also used some of them to wrap around his head, held in place with his underwear. It was quite a sight. I just assumed they were an extra pair; I was almost afraid to ask too many questions. When we are cold, we do whatever it takes to get warm.

One of the mottoes of the *Upward Basketball* program is doing "Whatever it Takes" to keep from turning children away. Shouldn't we be more fervent about introducing people to Christ than we are about our personal comfort?

Chapter 62

CRAPPIE FISHING AT SARDIS – *PERSUADED*

David Tutor and I went Crappie fishing at Sardis Lake one weekend. We had been there a few weeks before, fished almost all night long, and had worn out the Crappie in the spillway. If I remember right, on this particular trip we caught very few fish. Since the fish weren't biting and it was starting to rain, we turned in to the tent early. We had forgotten the poles for the tent so we tied the top center of the tent to a limb on a pine tree. We also used the fish dip net to help hold the tent off the ground. Thankfully, it was a warm night. When I woke up the next morning, the side of the tent was resting on my face. The water was soaking through the sidewall, and my sleeping bag was in about a half inch of water. We were miserable. After a short discussion, we slung everything in the back of the truck and went home.

Our decision to leave before the fishing trip was over was not a difficult one and was very insignificant. Either of us probably could have been persuaded to stay if the other one wanted. King Agrippa's decision when Paul told him the good news was not so inconsequential. "Then Agrippa said unto Paul, Almost thou persuadest me to be a Christian?" Acts 26:28. If you have been almost persuaded to turn your life over to Christ, please don't wait until it's too late.

Chapter 63

BB GUNS – DON'T SPOIL THE CHILD

I remember getting in trouble several times when I was a little chap. For instance, my brother and I had a matching pair of Daisy BB guns, and one time, my Mama caught us shooting at each other in the front yard. Barry was running across the yard. Mama came out the front door about the time I tagged him on the legs. They didn't shoot very hard but could have easily put an eye out. That was a stupid, stupid thing to do. I don't think my Mama ever spared the rod (a limb or belt usually replaced the rod).

Mama caught me once with my BB gun up against a tree. I knew the BB's would bounce off the tree, but I thought I could line it up where it would bounce back down the end of the barrel. I probably would have been glad if she let me in on the danger of it, without the punishment that went with her words.

Barry and I found a Blue Jay nest full of baby birds high up in a tree and used rocks to knock it down. It took us a long time. I can't even remember how Mama found out about it, and taking our BB guns away didn't seem like a fitting punishment for the crime at the time. Now I can understand how doing so got the point across.

"He that spareth his rod hateth his son: but he that loveth him chasteneth him betimes" Proverbs 13:24."Train up a child in the way he should go, and when he is old, he will not depart from it."
—Proverbs 22:6

Chapter 64

THE CREATION

What things or circumstances do you see or go through that make you remember we are not created by chance? For me, a few immediately come to mind: 1) newborn babies. 2) the top of clouds when viewed from an airplane—even when it is storming below. 3) there is a place just southwest of Springville I notice when coming home from work at sunset. I round the curve to a vast expanse of beautiful horizon filled with a mixture of orange, yellow, and pink clouds, with a blue or gray backdrop. It was painted by the Master's hands and given to me so that I can be in awe of its beauty. 4) the brightly burning embers deep inside a campfire mesmerize me. I can enjoy their warmth and beauty deep into the night.

"In the beginning God created the heaven and the earth" Genesis 1:1. Remember the things that you enjoy. Take comfort in the fact they were created by the One who is in control of all.

Chapter 65

FROG HUNTING – THE LIGHT

Back in the early 80's, we did a lot of frog hunting. One time, we went on an all-night frog hunting trip to Hatcher farm. The pools seemed alive at night when we added a light. There were three or four ponds and each one had a few frogs, snakes, and fish in them. For those of you who haven't been frog hunting, you know there are bullfrogs when you hear them. They moo like a cow. You can see the snakes and frogs around the edge of the pond.

We used a miniature pitchfork or gig to catch the frogs. The gig had a pole attached that was about ten feet long. We usually attached a cane pole, because it didn't weigh very much. Gigging was not difficult, but it was tricky. The light on the frog made it remain still. We were careful not to move the gig between the light and the frog, because the transition or shade would cause the frog to jump. We always got the gig to within a few inches of the frog or snake and then plunged it the last few inches. The lunge was the time to mess up. If I remember right, we gigged twenty-four frogs that night.

After you gig them, you have to run your hand down into the mud or water to the end of the gig and grab the frog before removing the gig. Before doing that we always checked to make sure there wasn't a snake beside it ready to eat the frog. After getting the frog in the boat, we stretched him out and cut his legs off. We pitched his upper body back into the water to feed the fish and turtles. If you weren't careful, the upper body would trick you into thinking it was another frog. Most of the twenty-four frogs had legs as big as chicken legs.

A good light made frog hunting a lot better. The spider webs shined in the dew and light. Snakes in the limbs were easier to see. It was much better to see them on the limbs than it was for them to fall in the boat with us. The better the light, the more the bugs were attracted to us. Sometimes the fish would jump toward the light—even jumping into the boat.

> Just like with the frogs, if we let shadows come between us and the light, we lose our focus and are apt to jump in any direction. Like the bugs and the fish, we should be attracted to the light. "Then spake Jesus again unto them, saying, I am the light of the world:

he that followeth me shall not walk in darkness, but shall have the light of life"

—John 8:12

Chapter 66

SOYBEAN FIELD FIGHTS – INTENTIONS

B ack when we farmed soybeans, I had to help get the bags ready and help fill the hoppers of the planters with soybeans. When I was twelve, my job was to move the five-speed ton truck fifty or sixty yards down the field to keep up with the planters. My cousins and I had time to kill in between loading the planters. One of our pastimes involved using the empty soybean sacks as shields in dirt clod fights. If you positioned yourself just right, you could almost hide behind the sack. If there were more than two people fighting, it was almost impossible to hide. If you threw a big enough dirt clod hard enough, you could knock the sack out of their hands. Then there was just a few seconds with no protection, almost like a disabled force field. It was a lot of fun but usually ended with someone getting hurt or mad.

Our anger wasn't premeditated. When Cain killed Abel, I wonder if it was premeditated. When they went into the field, do you think Cain's intention could have been to discuss the situation?

Chapter 67

SHOOTING AT DOE BEHIND ROLO'S — *ANTICIPATION*

One time, we went deer hunting with the beagles up near my Uncle Mike's. The beagles bumped around a bit, but couldn't seem to get anything going. Chet and I went to cousin Rolo's house and set out behind it overlooking a grass bottom with hardwoods on the other side. We were downwind from the beagles, but up on a high ridge so we could hear pretty well. The dogs jumped a deer up hot and sounded like they were headed our way.

When the dogs are coming my way, I guess my nerves get a little jumpy, because I always need to use the bathroom even if I have just used it. My son never seems to get excited, but things were a little different this day. The dogs kept getting closer and we could hear them coming down through the hardwoods on the other ridge. Chet

159

had his 410 with buckshot and I had a 270. We had worked it out where if it was a doe, he was going to shoot it. If it was a buck, we both were going to shoot it. The big doe jumped out only a few yards in front of the dogs. She was one hundred and fifty yards from us and turned running broadside to our right down by the creek in the bottom. Chet fired. He looked to me to give him another shot shell, which I didn't have. He set the gun down and took off running for the truck to get another shell. His hurry turned into a fall as his body got going faster than his legs and feet. When he returned with another shell, he wanted to know if I thought he hit the deer. I told him it was possible but not very likely since it was so far away. We went and looked for blood but didn't find any.

> I have seen Chet excited before but never more so than that day. "But let the righteous be glad; let them rejoice before God: yea, let them exceedingly rejoice" Psalm 68:3. As I think about how my anticipation and excitement rises when the dogs are getting close, I wonder about the people Isaiah spoke to about the coming birth of Christ. Might they have been excited about it seven hundred plus years before the event? "For unto us a child is born, unto us a son is given: and the government shall be upon his shoulder: and his name shall be called Wonderful, Counselor, The Mighty God, The Everlasting Father, The Prince of Peace."
>
> —Isaiah 9:6

Chapter 68

SHOP HUNTING – FOR SHOW

Once I was working in the shop on something and heard hounds howling. I grabbed my rifle and went outside. This had happened once before and I had killed a doe between the shop and the highway. On this particular day the dogs were behind the shop. I waited a short while and two does jumped out of the woods and ran across the back yard broadside to me. I let them go and later had second thoughts about it.

The single tree where we hang deer was on the back of my shop. It had a small wench for cranking the deer up in the air. The part that attaches to the deer was home made. We had to go back and add an additional leg to it, because I had to break the deer legs to get them spread out far enough to mount on the single tree. After much shame (thinking my deer were so small), I later found out that it was also too large for very big deer.

I sometimes wish I had shot one of the deer, because I think it would have been close enough that I could have hooked the single tree to it and never dragged it or picked it up. That would have been something to talk about! The truth of the matter is they were running fast enough that I probably couldn't have hit one of them anyway.

In Luke chapter 18, Jesus tells a story of a Pharisee and a publican praying. The Pharisee brags on himself telling of his accomplishments and the faults of the publican. The publican asks for mercy as a sinner. Jesus spoke of the publican. "I tell you, this man went down to his house justified rather than the other: for every one that exalteth himself shall be abased; and he that humbleth himself shall be exalted."

—Luke 18:14

Chapter 69

WALKING
THE BIG DITCH –
ARMOR

G ranny would sometimes tell us about farming in the bottom behind her house. When Mama was an infant, Granny would put her on a pallet beside the big ditch while she and my granddaddy were working in the field. Sometimes we (my brother and I) would talk Mama into letting us walk the same ditch and we would go barefooted or with rubber boots. We would have to cross roots and trees and little pools that were always deeper than our boots.

Shells were one of my favorite things to look at and collect in the ditch. I thought they had to be thousands of years old. We regularly got tangled up in the vines. One of our goals was to find a "Tarzan vine." We knew if we could swing all the way across the ditch, it was a good one. It was very perplexing that our grapevines

163

were always attached at the ground—unlike Tarzan's. As I am sitting in a shooting house now overlooking a food plot, I can hear the trickle of water from a nearby stream that feeds the big ditch a couple of hundred yards from here. My mind is wandering down the ditch that we walked as kids. Thinking back now, we probably should have worn snake chaps and steel toed shoes! We never got seriously hurt.

> When thinking about snake chaps, I am reminded of the armor of God. Ephesians 6:10-11 tells us, "Finally, my brethren, be strong in the Lord, and in the power of his might. Put on the whole armour of God, that ye may be able to stand against the wiles of the devil."

Chapter 70

WALKING IN THE MOUNTAINS OF SWITZERLAND, A PSALM OF PRAISE

O Lord, the pine trees at the foot of the mountains take me back home. The narrow winding trail that goes up the mountain is a reminder of the way things were before four-wheelers and vehicles and telephones. Lord, thank you for this moment in your basic creation; as I look at the cattle water troughs filled by the streams, I'm reminded of your provision for me. Weather huts built hundreds of years ago offer a place of shelter in times of need.

Music of the cowbells is so peaceful it almost seems like it is from an instrument.

Lord you ensure my footing as I view the deep escarpments when a slip or a wrong turn could mean sudden death. Pictures cannot capture half the beauty. The grassy meadows scattered along the side of the mountain give a feeling of pure peacefulness and calm that I get even when looking back at the pictures.

As we search for the fabled Edelweiss and find only the beautiful Encion, I think of Solomon and his array. Lord, the beauty of the flowers is indescribable. Lord, how good you are to me blessing me with the ability and the opportunity to take a walk covering eight miles and three thousand vertical feet. Thin air at the snow line causes me to slow and enjoy.

The crystal clear lake at the snowline starts my mind racing with questions about depth and temperature and kinds of fish. As I view the shining quartz rocks and boulders through the clear water and all around the lake, I wish only for the perfect rock to take home to my family.

Snow peaks touching the clouds seem to point at the power of God: the only thing more awesome to look at would be the angelic choir announcing the birth of Christ to the shepherds. One of these millennium, I want to see a rerun of that performance.

Chapter 71

THE WELL - FRUSTRATION

When studying about Isaac and the trouble he had with wells in Genesis chapter 26, I think about the well in the back pasture behind my Granny's house. In all the years I roamed those hills, we never used it for water, only for a place to put stuff. We put dirt, dead animals, brush, and rubbish in it quite often and never seemed to fill it up. When the Philistines stopped up Isaac's wells it must have been no small task. I wonder what they were thinking because they must have wanted to use it after Isaac was gone.

Barry, Brian, Rolo, and I took a short walk through the hardwood thicket below the well (it seems like you would dig a well down in the holler instead of on top of the hill). If I remember right, Brian and I walked through the hardwoods, while Barry was in the lower pasture and Rolo was in the pasture on the hill. We had seen a lot of buck sign in the hardwoods so we were excited to see what we could run out. About half way through, a deer jumped up between me and Brian and went back toward where we started. It managed to run fast enough and stay in the thicket and behind trees so we couldn't get a clear shot. I think we took a couple of shots anyway, but that sounded like a reasonable enough excuse for missing it.

We started yelling at Rolo, "It is going back toward the power line." Rolo took off running. He ran back past the well to where he could see in the power line. He took a shot or two when the deer came out. His excuse was that he had run so hard and was breathing so hard that the cross hairs of his scope were going up and down with every breath and he couldn't hold it on the deer.

The frustration that Isaac had with having to move around so much must have been immense in comparison to Rolo's frustration. Isaac chose peace and God blessed him richly.

Chapter 72

DEERING –

FISHERS OF DEER

On 12/27/04, several of us went deer hunting behind my Granny Westmoreland's house. I got there late—about 8:45 a.m. They had already jumped three does out of one thicket. The beagles had run them by one of the guys and he couldn't shoot, because the sun was too bright in his scope. I parked about halfway up the big hill just above my dad's food plot going toward the old well. The dog race had broken up and there were just a few puppies barking.

Suddenly, there were a few shots down in the bottom. One of the guys said on the walkie-talkie there were two does and a good buck going across the bottom and into the woods. Two of the deer were going one way and one was going the other. I cranked up and headed fast toward the two, because it sounded like they would come out in the open. I later found out that the buck was headed toward where I was parked. I got back there just in time to see the dogs cross the field road between two hardwood blocks about fifty yards from where I was located in the beginning. Shortly after that I heard three shots (my brother). He came on the radio and said the deer was a good buck and was headed toward the apple orchard.

The race was on to get in shooting position. When I got to the power line and got stopped, there were two others arriving at the same time. The guy up next to the race came on the radio and said he was headed north toward the power line. We got a good rest and prepared to shoot. We could see seven or eight hundred yards on the power line. My fear was that it would come across in one of the valleys where we couldn't see it. Seconds later, there were several shots a hundred and fifty yards or so south of us. We later found out the deer was headed directly toward us, but was going to come out within twenty-five yards of us. The deer had run across a kudzu patch going down the hill toward a pond. Gable Todd shot it running through the kudzu. It went down the hill and into the ice-covered pond. As it was breaking ice and jumping over a log in the pond, he shot it again. It swam out toward the middle of the pond and took its last breath. My brother and Gable said its nose was the last thing to go under. The beagles were crawling out on the log trying to find the deer.

My dad found a three-prong hook that weighed about twenty pounds and about fifty feet of rope. We spent about an hour and a half dragging the pond with the hook. The pond was only about a quarter of an acre so we were amazed that the deer was difficult to find. The hook was awkward and cumbersome to throw. It should be an easier place to fish now, because of all the logs that were dragged out of the way. I was wishing the whole time that my son was with us. I am sure he would have volunteered to go in after it—at least until he touched the water.

We went back hunting and ran at least two more deer with my brother killing one of them. In the meantime my dad was welding some poles together and putting a hook on the end to make it better for probing. We took the boat over to the pond. A couple of the guys began probing around for the deer. The water was about eight feet deep where they thought the deer went under. After trying that for a while they dropped the hook behind the boat and we dragged the boat across the pool pulling the hook behind it. Still no success. We gave up.

> As with so many times before, I left too soon and the action was right where I had started. Don't we sometimes think that we need to be somewhere else before God can use us? "And he saith unto them, Follow me, and I will make you fishers of men."
> —Mathew 4:19

Chapter 73

EIGHT DEER -
DECEPTION

Several of us went hunting in Pontotoc, MS, on New Year's Eve. We were hunting cutover and pine thickets with beagles. The most interesting stories were about the deer that we missed. Someone counted up about nineteen that we didn't get. We killed eight deer that day. There were five does and three small bucks. We took pictures at the end of the day. Several of us pulled a good rack of antlers out of the back of our pickup trucks and used them to make the picture a lot more interesting. We all thought it would be humorous to deceive everyone about how successful our hunt had been by making the does look like big bucks. I wonder how many city folks carry antlers around in the back of their pickup?

We turned the beagles loose in the one cutover thicket we could get around. I went to the bottom of the hill next to a beaver slough. The beagles jumped and began hammering down the hill right toward me. I pushed the safety off on my shotgun and got ready. Suddenly the preacher shot five times just around the curve from me. Deer started shooting across the four-wheeler trail I was on. I got two shots off at the last two. The beagles came across within seconds. A minute or so later there were two or three more shots on top of the next hill. The guy there said on the radio there were two does and a big buck. The preacher and I thought they were all does which meant at least two had been traded off for the big buck within about two or three hundred yards—either that or we had got two of them. We began the search.

The problem with shooting buckshot is it often doesn't bring the deer down immediately.

We didn't find them. I had both guns on the four-wheeler, so I traded the shotgun for my rifle.

A little while later several of us were on top of the hill listening to the beagles quite a long ways off hoping they were coming back our way. I stepped out into the pasture about twenty yards in front of the other guys. I noticed a doe about forty yards down the hill walking to my right. I put the cross hairs on her chest and shot at her through the sage grass. She took off and I took another shot at her. A buck jumped up beside her and took off.

I shot at him too. He went over the hill and another guy killed him. The doe only went about twenty yards. When I looked back, my brother who was behind me said, "You need to let us know when something comes out so we can all shoot!" We all knew that was a joke.

Jacob deceived his father Isaac and stole his brother's birthright. Of course there was strife between Jacob and his brother for a long time. I sometimes wonder if the terrible things that happened with Joseph and his brothers were also a consequence of Jacob's deception. God used it to bring about good in the end, with Joseph being second in command in Egypt. But you know that God could have made that happen without all the turmoil!

Chapter 74

RABBITS IN THE TUB –
ANGER

We went rabbit hunting once in Grenada and harvested a bunch of rabbits. In one race, Sissy and Fluffy ran a few circles with a big swamp rabbit. The rabbit came down off a hardwood hill and my brother couldn't shoot it, because the dogs were too close. They caught the rabbit going down the hill. Sometimes there was a good argument over who got to count the rabbit when the dogs caught it.

When we got home and cleaned the rabbits, it was very cold outside and we didn't want to wash them outdoors. We decided to wash them in the bathtub, which seemed like the natural thing to do. My Granny always fussed if we brought her a rabbit that had hair on it. She told us, "Just bring it whole if you ain't going to do any better than that." The secret to dressing a rabbit is not getting the hair on it to start with. We got the rabbits in the tub and forgot about them or maybe we just had something else we needed to do. When my mama saw the rabbits in the tub, I don't think anger is a sufficient description! I don't remember what our punishment was, but Mama controlled her anger.

> I believe that Jesus was angry when he made the moneychangers and merchants leave the temple. Won't it be great one day to know exactly how that event took place? I think there are a lot of other things happening now that God wants us to get angry about. "Be ye angry and sin not:"
> —Ephesians 4:26a

Chapter 75

SAWMILL HOLLER – A MERRY HEART

We were hunting at Calhoun on the game area when I was a kid. I really enjoyed hunting with all my family there. We didn't kill a lot of deer. We saw a lot of deer but female deer were not legal game. Sawmill holler was filled with thick five to ten-year-old pines with some larger pines mixed in. As I write this it has been cut, reset, and has five to ten-year-old pines on it again. There were also some sparse hardwoods on the south end.

I was in the hardwoods one morning as the dogs were headed in my direction. I was about halfway down a ridge and thought I heard the deer coming, then I held my rifle up just as the deer were coming down the hill right at me. They were in a single file line. There were eight deer and they each got within about twenty-five

179

feet before they saw me. It almost seemed like they had worked it out ahead of time, because they were taking turns peeling off to the right and then left and then right and then left. Eight deer and no antlers in the bunch! Of course I would have liked for them all to be bucks, but I was glad to see deer.

> Deer camp for us wasn't all about killing deer. It was about fellowship, nature, four wheel drives, muddy roads, card games, looking for dogs, good food, and family. Even considering the very few deer that I harvested, I enjoyed my youth at deer camp. "A merry heart doeth good like a medicine: but a broken spirit drieth the bones."
>
> —Proverbs 17:22

Chapter 76

BOBCAT AT NOXUBEE – FEAR

I heard a bobcat scream once when we were rabbit hunting. It sounded so much like a person that I felt like my blood was curdling.

I had a tree stand for deer hunting across the river on the Noxubee refuge. The prior week I had been bowhunting and saw three deer. They came up about fifty yards from me, but no closer. They were on the trail coming toward me so I didn't dare take a shot. As I was standing up in my ladder stand, my nerves got the better of me. My right leg started shaking and I couldn't get it to stop. I am sure now that it wasn't, but it felt like it was shaking the entire tree, which obviously would scare the deer away. I twiddled my toes and tried to think of other things to get it to stop. I jammed it against the stand as hard as I could. Almost saving me embarrassment the deer meandered off in another direction.

On this particular trip I didn't see any deer. But at primetime a few minutes before dark, a bobcat came sauntering down the same trail the deer had been on the week before. He was a big one. I prepared to draw, but decided against it because I didn't want to lose the chance of a deer coming by. It was the perfect time! A few minutes later I began to ponder the fact the bobcat had walked down the same trail that I had to walk to get back to the river and then to the truck. I had to walk toward him to leave! I thought about the one I had heard scream. Chills went down my spine. I am sure a little bitty light like I had has never worked harder looking over the woods than on that trip back to the truck.

God can take our fears and worries and melt them into a peace that passes all understanding—if we allow him. He is in control. "God is our refuge and strength, a very present help in trouble."

—Psalm 46:1

Chapter 77

ROADKILL – *SLUGGARD*

We were pulling lines to start building our house when we heard tires skidding and a loud crash like a tire blowing out. We went down to the highway a few hundred yards away and saw a neighbor who had run into the last of five deer. She didn't want the deer so we got it. There was nothing bruised but the front shoulder of the deer—and the car!

Jan and I ran over a rabbit one night on the way to my brother-in-law's house. We stopped and got it. Nothing is better than rabbit backbone.

We were coming home from church one Wednesday night, and an eight-point buck was lurking in the road ditch beside the road. Just as I got beside him, he lunged across the road. I slammed on the brakes and tried to dodge him, but hit him. His head centered my grill with one antler flying across to my right. The deer spun down the road behind me. We backed up and loaded him up. There was no meat ruined below the neck. Deer is one of our favorite foods.

> God provided manna and quail for the Israelites in the wilderness. He provides for me in many ways. This provision only requires me to work a little to receive it. "Go to the ant, thou sluggard; consider her ways, and be wise: Which having no guide, overseer, or ruler, Provideth her meat in the summer, and gathereth her food in the harvest."
>
> —Proverbs 6:6-8

Chapter 78

DADDY SHOWED US UP – HONOR

Several of us went fishing at Joe Kidd's pond across highway nine from the City Lake road. It was me, Daddy, Barry, and either Mitch or Ashley. Four of us were in the ten-foot aluminum boat fishing in a pond that you could almost cast across. The pool was muddy and shallow everywhere except along the levee. We knew there were some fish in it, because they were making waves in the shallows. We fished for a while and caught a couple of small bass on the standard worms and topwater baits. Then we hit a dry spell. We fished with quite a few different lures with no success. Daddy pulled out an old red plastic worm with three hooks in it and some little red and yellow balls with holes in them on the leader. It must have been twenty years old at the time. He tied it on and began to cast. After he caught a pretty nice four or five pounder, we began digging through the tackle boxes for a red plastic worm. He caught one or two more before he caught the big one. We all just sat back and watched as dad taught the kind of lesson he always told everyone he gave us when usually he didn't.

> Watching my dad and the way he cares for my grandparents makes me realize how much influence my treatment of Jan's and my parents can have on my kids. "Honor thy father and thy mother: that thy days may be long upon the land which the Lord thy God giveth thee."
>
> —Exodus 20:12

Chapter 79

TWO DEER —
CHOOSE WISELY

I spent one winter after deer season trying to lose a few pounds by running a chainsaw behind my house. I cleared out some food plots going in three different directions from a spot I thought would be a good place for a deer stand. I went two hundred and fifty yards north, one hundred and fifty yards southwest and one hundred and fifty yards west. I cleared the path wide enough to get a tractor between the trees and wider where I didn't have to cut any hardwoods. Chet and I spent a Saturday building a shooting house that was four by six feet with a roof and a carpet floor. My Paslode Cordless Framing Nailer was a treestand builder's dream-come-true.

When deer season rolled around, I was ready to try it out. I had planted clover, rye grass, and oats. Chet was sick so I went by myself on the Tuesday before

Thanksgiving 2002. At about 8:15 a.m. a deer stepped out in my food plot on the north side of the tree house. It was a doe and didn't look very big. The thought of my kids in the house wanting deer meat every meal they can talk me into cooking it made me willing to harvest it. It was eating clover so I decided to wait and see if another would come out.

A few minutes later two more deer stepped into the food plot. They were approximately one hundred yards away so I moved my sandbag to the north side of the tree house. I took aim at the largest one and then cranked my scope up to full power. I put the crosshairs on her chest and squeezed the trigger. When I looked up the deer was lying on the ground kicking. I got down and walked to where she was and saw that it was a small deer. I thought I must have pulled off the bigger doe when I cranked the power up on the scope. Then I noticed she was shot in the head. Not only had I shot the wrong deer, I had almost missed her! What an awful feeling. I took her back to the house and skinned her out.

While I was working on her I really got frustrated wondering how I could have missed the bigger deer. The thought crossed my mind that I could have shot through the first one and hit one of the others. I took my bloodhound to where the deer was lying and he went about forty yards back into the woods to where the first deer was lying shot through the heart.

In this story I made some bad choices. First, I made food plots long and narrow such that multiple deer would most likely be lined up. Second, I did not pay close enough attention to what was behind where I was shooting.

On the next Tuesday before Thanksgiving 2003, I made a couple of more bad decisions. I was in the same tree stand reading a book. I looked up to see a six or eight point running away from me at about one hundred and thirty yards in the west food plot. I dropped the book, grabbed my rifle, and aimed thinking he would stop. He didn't stop. He turned, trotting out of the food plot. I took a quick shot before he made it out. He spun around allowing me to get off another shot before he hopped out of the food plot going north.

While I was sitting there thinking I either needed to be hunting or reading a book (because the deer may have been out there grazing before I saw him), a deer stepped into sight about sixty or seventy yards into the hardwoods past where the first deer appeared. I scoped it and could only see about six inches of the deer right behind its front shoulder. It was behind two trees. It looked like a big deer, but was coming from the same direction the first one came from. The first deer would have had to make a big circle to show up like this. I thought it was either the first deer or a big doe. Either way I wanted the meat. I decided to take the shot. I squeezed the trigger and the deer hit the ground. It was a small buck—neither of the two options that I had considered. Rusty (the bloodhound) and I trailed the first deer for a half-mile or so without finding any blood before giving up.

> We should take time to think about what we are doing or saying in almost every situation. Daniel and his friends gave us some good examples of choosing wisely. They were concerned about food but not with losing weight! They negotiated with their captors and proved to them that God's way was better than the Babylonian way. Their choice could have very easily been death or the Babylonian way. When it comes down to clutch time—as when they were facing the fiery furnace—we have to be willing to make the tough decisions just like they did.

Chapter 80

OLD LUKE – LYING

Luke was the last bird dog that my dad trained. I keep thinking he is going to get another, but he hasn't yet. He was a long-haired setter and was one of the best when he was a young dog. A few years ago, my brother-in-law Brian and I borrowed him to make a deer drive. We had made the same drive a year before and spooked five or six deer out. I had knocked a doe down at over three hundred yards running with iron sights. Thinking back, I probably hit the deer behind the one I was shooting at. A good bird dog doesn't run a deer like a deer dog. But sometimes they trail them enough to spook them out. A person walking through the woods might not jump a bedded deer unless he gets very close. If he does jump the deer sometimes he doesn't know and doesn't follow the trail close enough to spook them out. The scent from a deer is so strong that a bird dog can't help himself following for a short piece.

Luke had gotten older but we took him hunting anyway. We went down beside the beaver slough and started into the woods. The briars were over our heads, so we were kind of hoping that Luke would do the tough walking for us. He went about twenty yards into the briar thicket and pointed. We couldn't get him to move so I went in to flush whatever he was pointing. I thought the briars were going to punch through my boots as I lifted my leg as high as it would go and then rode the briars down trying to get to him. I had to go all the way to him and flush a woodcock that was right in front of his nose.

We walked three-or-four-hundred yards through some pretty thick stuff although it wasn't as bad as it was initially. We didn't see a deer and we started missing Luke about halfway through the trip. We thought he might have been pointed somewhere and were dreading going back through looking for him. When we got back to the truck Luke was lying down resting by the tailgate. Not only did Luke tell the truth when he pointed, he didn't play any games about his physical condition.

Sometimes it is very difficult to tell the truth when you are tired and give out. You want to lie down and finish having your heart failure, but you keep walking because it seems like the manly thing to do.

192

Jeremiah told the truth to King Zedekiah even when it meant risking his life. This story is told in Jeremiah chapters 37 and 38. "Wherefore putting away lying, speaking every man truth with his neighbour: for we are members one of another."

—Ephesians 4:24

Chapter 81

OPOSSUM –
THE GOOD? THE BAD? &
THE UGLY!

Several of us went muzzleloader deer hunting on an island in the Tombigbee Waterway. I took a standing position on one end of the island while a couple of the other guys meandered around. While I was leaning against a tree waiting, I saw a possum coming toward me. It was easing along staying out in front of one of the guys walking. As it got closer, I decided that I was going to scare it. When it got close to me, I jumped away from the tree toward the possum. I screamed in a loud roaring growl as I hit the ground in front of him. When I did, he sort of leaned to one side and showed all his teeth and growled back for a split second. For those of you who haven't seen a possum, the length of the mouth and head is about a third of the length of the entire animal. It is about as ugly and mean of a sight as you can imagine. He then instantly ran toward my right leg. He jumped around my leg and into a hole in the ground behind my right foot. Who do you think got scared in this situation?

> The possum was intent on getting into the hole. He may have been on his way to see his ugly little possum girlfriend that his wife didn't know about. He could have been on his way home to his family who was waiting scared inside the den. He was a very determined possum either to do wrong or right. "If we say that we have no sin, we deceive ourselves, and the truth is not in us. If we confess our sins, he is faithful and just to forgive us our sins, and to cleanse us from all unrighteousness."
>
> —1 John 1:8, 9

Chapter 82

THE MAP – BIBLE

We used to think we fished almost every accessible lake or pond in the county. We always threatened to, but never did take a county map and label and number all the lakes. We were going to journal information about each one of them. There were so many that you could easily forget important things about them. A few examples:

- Bird Malden's pond was always good for a stringer of small bass. No one I knew of ever caught a big one there. It took a four-wheel drive to get to it. Now houses surround it.
- Uncle George's was always good for one or two big healthy bass. It was a nightmare to try to access.
- The Natchez Trace Lake had big bass. They would always bite a plastic worm, but sometimes

it was hard to catch them. Entirely too many people fished there.

- There was a lake at Randolph that was good for fishing, but the person that gave us permission might run us off with a shotgun. We had to catch her in the right mood.
- Jacob's watershed was one of the best, but you had to go with someone who he gave permission to fish. The only person I could go with was a veterinarian who worked on his cows.
- Center Hill had a small but deep pond in the bottom of a cutover. The fish were kind of pale. It always seemed like there was potential there for a monster. It was also sheltered from the wind.
- Troy had three or four really nice watershed lakes. Some of them were difficult to get into. The ones that weren't were fished often by many folks.
- Lafayette Springs, which was just across the county line, had a couple of nice watershed lakes. The water was shallow and you needed a depth finder to stay in the creek that ran through the middle of the lake.

The Bible was given to us for some reasons similar to the ones we were thinking about with our journal. First, it is a map that shows us where to go. Second, the journal gives us vital information in determining what we should to do next. When Josiah heard about the scroll the priest had found, it convicted his heart. "And it came to pass, when the king had heard the words of the book of the law, that he rent his clothes" 2 Kings 23:11. "Lead me in thy truth, and teach me."

—Psalm 25:5a

Chapter 83

FIRST DEER
WITH BOW –
DON'T GIVE UP

Gary Higgins and I were hunting in some hard-woods in the middle of the game area in Calhoun County. He had found a white oak that must have had very sweet acorns, because the deer kept coming back to it. I climbed a white oak about one hundred yards from Gary's tree to hunt one afternoon. I saw squirrels all afternoon and turned around in my stand many times thinking a squirrel sounded like a deer. I gave up on the squirrels and relaxed. At 5:55 p.m. a doe appeared to my left about ten yards from the base of my tree. It had fed all the way to me, but I thought it was a squirrel. I drew and released. The deer slammed into a tree and ran off down the hill out of sight.

I climbed out of the tree, retrieved my arrow (with blood on it), and went to find Gary. It was dark by this time. We went to Calhoun City for supper so the deer had time to bleed out. We returned a couple of hours later and began to trail it. We spent a lot of time on our hands and knees finding only a spec of blood every few feet. We trailed for a couple more hours getting turned around and somewhat lost in a pine thicket. Lost is a tricky term, because we were in an area where the main road was always at the highest point. We gave up when we couldn't find any more blood. When we started for the highest point, we found we were only about one hundred yards from the main road. The next week was opening weekend of gun season. I decided to see if I could find the spot where we last saw the deer. In the daylight, I quickly found the stump where we had marked the last blood. A quick scan around revealed the deer lying about twenty yards from where we had trailed her. We shouldn't have given up.

> My father-in-law was a good example of not giving up. He went blind the last few years, had cancer, and died with pneumonia well past his ninetieth birthday. His attitude was good until the end. "Wait on the Lord: be of good courage, and he shall strengthen thine heart: wait, I say, on the Lord: Psalm 27:14."But they that wait upon the Lord shall renew their strength; they shall mount up with wings as eagles; they shall run, and not be weary; and they shall walk, and not faint."
>
> —Isaiah 40:31

Chapter 84

MUZZLELOADER DOE
BEHIND HOUSE –
GREEDY

One Saturday afternoon Jan was fussing about something, so I went to my treestand about 4:30 p.m. I dozed off in my lawn chair and woke up with three deer in the food plot next to the stand. I picked up my musket and eased it up through the stand window while trying to gather my composure. I focused the sights on the largest deer and squeezed the trigger. It was difficult to see clearly through the smoke but I thought one deer went straight ahead and the others went the opposite way. I began reloading as the two deer stepped back out into the food plot. I tried to hide and hurry at the same time. I eased the gun back out the window and focused on the biggest deer again. The thought occurred to me that I really couldn't see how I missed the first deer. I decided not to shoot. When I got down and went to look, the first deer had fallen just barely out of sight. When I tried to unload my gun (by shooting it), I found that I had forgotten to put a cap in it. I only thought I could have shot the second deer!

> Sometimes we want more and more and don't know when to stop wanting. My competitive nature makes life a daily struggle in this area. "For the love of money is the root of all evil."
> —1 Timothy 6:10a

Chapter 85

BOW FROGGING –
BEFORE AND AFTER

B ack when we really got into bow hunting deer, in
1990, we used the off-season to hone our skills
shooting other things. We did some crazy things prac-
ticing. Once, we put a ladder on top of a picnic table.
We wanted to work on shooting from a strained balance
position while in the air. Today, we would call that an
"unsafe condition caused by an unsafe act!" We also
practiced from sixty to seventy yards. We lost a lot of arrows. We also tried shooting frogs with very little success.
The problem was with placement of the frogs. Too many
times they were out in the water with no backstop. We
could use a recurve with a reel on it but it wasn't very
accurate and didn't give us the practice we wanted with
our compound bows. I once took a picture of a frog,

shot it, and then took another picture. I can't remember why I wanted a before and after picture.

> If you have already committed your life to Christ, think back to that day. Could someone watching you tell the difference between before and after? "When I was a child, I spake as a child, I understood as a child, I thought as a child: but when I became a man, I put away childish things"
>
> —1 Corinthians 13:11

Chapter 86

BOW FISHING – CONSIDERATION

S hortly after Jan and I got married, Scott Hatcher and I went bow fishing. I don't remember very much about the fishing trip. It was before cell phones were common. I remember thinking sometime during the night that I wished I was close to a phone so I could let Jan know where I was and it would be very late before I got home. When I got home the next morning, there was a considerable amount of my clothes strewn about the yard. Needless to say, she was very angry with me. I should have shown more consideration.

> "And let us consider one another to provoke unto love and to good works."
> —Hebrews 10:24

Chapter 87

ROAD DITCH FIGHTS – LIMITATIONS

I was recently reminded of the wrestling matches we used to have at deer camp. We were hunting at the county line when my cousin's two boys got into a good scrap. They rolled around in the road ditch until they were both almost too tired to get up.

About twenty years ago another cousin was riding with me at deer camp. I got in the truck and started it up. The radio almost busted my eardrums! Someone had turned the volume all the way up. I looked at my cousin and said, "Get out." He replied, "I ain't the same little boy I used to be." After about four rolls in the road ditch, he decided that he hadn't outgrown me—yet.

The most fun fights to watch were the ones when one of my cousins would challenge one of my uncles and my uncles were too proud to admit that they were too old and out of shape to be fighting. We should know our limitations.

> We should also know that we aren't limited when we are doing what God wants us to do. "One man of you shall chase a thousand: for the Lord your God, he it is that fightieth for you, as he hath promised you."
> —Joshua 23:10

Chapter 88

ONE HORNED DEER — LEADERS

I was hunting at a neighbor's one morning and didn't see anything. As I was leaving I heard some beagles getting close and running hard. I stepped away from the truck and out into a pasture. I saw the deer appear on the other side of a pond one hundred and seventy yards away and stop behind a tree. He was a one horned buck and would have to cross the pasture if he stayed on the same course. I hit a knee and waited. The dogs were getting closer so I suspected he was about to bolt across the pasture. He did. I started swinging my rifle with the deer. When I crossed his chest with the crosshairs of the scope, I squeezed the trigger. He plowed the ground when his nose hit. He rolled and came up running. I took another shot and he kept going. The beagles came out and followed his trail out of sight. I listened to them for a while until they went out of hearing. When I got home I did some quick calculating. My bullet probably hit the deer in the hindquarter. Based on the calculations using the speed of the deer, the distance to him, and the muzzle velocity of the bullet I should have aimed 2.3 feet in front of where I wanted to hit. I should have remembered that I needed to lead the deer at such a distance.

Bird hunting with a shotgun is the same. Sometimes doves are flying at sixty miles per hour. You have to get out in front of them several feet, depending on how far away they are. It is even trickier with a bow and arrow because the arrow speed is so slow.

Joshua tried to lead the people into the land of Canaan that God had promised them. He was following God's lead. We should be careful who we allow to lead us. Jesus spoke of the Pharisees: "Let them alone: they be blind leaders of the blind. And if the blind lead the blind, both shall fall into the ditch."

—Matthew 15:14

Chapter 89

ROTTEN EGG HAILSTORM – *STRENGTH*

When I was little, we were down at the fishpond at my Granny's. We got out in the boat and paddled around picking blackberries and playing in the water with the paddle. We found a duck nest on the edge of the lake that was full of eggs. We grabbed a few of them and, as kids sometimes do, we dropped one of them. The eggs must have been there a long time because there was such a rotten, foul stench! It wasn't long after the egg hit the bottom of the boat that we piled out of the boat and into the water leaving the egg to make it on its own.

Another time at the pool when we were even smaller, a sudden hailstorm came up. My dad turned the boat over and held it up so we could get under it. I have a perfect mental picture of the hail, because it was shaped like candy corn with a little white tip on the end.

Isaiah was praising our heavenly Father in Isaiah 25:4: "For thou hast been a strength to the poor, a strength to the needy in his distress, a refuge from the storm, a shadow from the heat, when the blast of the terrible ones is as a storm against the wall."

Chapter 90

TWO BOW HUNTS –
HIGH PLACES

I went bow hunting with Gary at Airmount. I had not been there before, so I relied on him to get me in the general vicinity of a good spot. He sent me in one direction, while he went in another. I went to the creek as he had directed and found a good-looking spot overlooking a trail running along the creek at a crossing. There was a ridge about twenty feet above the creek. I found a good tree to climb on the ridge and got ready. I was only about fifteen feet up the tree, which put me about thirty-five feet above the top edge of the creek. I thought I was in excellent position. After I had sat there for a while I heard something. Three deer were coming—not down the creek as I expected, but down the hill from above me. As the first deer got within about twenty yards of me, it stepped behind a tree, which would have been perfect if not for the other two deer coming along behind it. I had to draw and by this time the deer were at eye level. I knew I couldn't wait, because they were coming straight for me and would only see me better as they came closer. I was just hoping the first one would hold even if the other two bolted. It didn't. They ran back out the same trail they came in.

On another bow hunting trip, I went to the game area in Calhoun County. I climbed a big Oak in the bottom of a streamside management area left by a timber company. It was nestled between two cutovers with a high cliff on one side and a creek on the other and lots of acorns underneath. I figured if anything came by on my side of the creek it would have to come within shooting distance.

After hunting a little while I noticed a deer moving through the thicket underneath a White Oak on the other side of the creek. I could have taken a shot, but decided it was too difficult and they might ease on toward me. Minutes later I heard a deer hit the creek that was only about ten yards from the base of my tree. I was twenty-five feet up the tree, with the tree between the deer and me. I was in good position, but further review revealed the deer was more to the left side of the tree than to the right. I had to move my bow around to the other side of the tree and draw without making a sound. It was a big doe and she was feeding underneath the tree I was in.

I started easing my bow to the other side between the tree and me. I was almost there when deer started hitting the creek to my right. There were two small deer in the creek playing and another large doe on the other side coming into the creek. They were all only ten to fifteen yards away. As I couldn't figure a good way to get the shot off at the first deer and the others were coming in perfect, I moved back to that side. When the deer started up out of the creek toward me, she was naturally looking up out of the creek and spotted me on the side of the tree. She froze. I froze. She stepped back down into the creek and turned broadside. I thought, "It's now or never." I drew and got my sight on her just before she jumped out of the creek on the other side. I was so close but didn't release. They all ran away quickly. The two smaller deer got separated from the two larger ones with me in between. I listened to them run back and forth looking for each other for the next thirty minutes. The larger deer would blow at the smaller ones. The smaller ones would just run around searching.

The devil tempted Jesus in high places, Matthew 4:1-11. No matter how high in a treestand you are, you can still be seen in certain circumstances. Satan may come after you when you are at a high point in your life. We should hide the Scriptures in our heart just like Jesus did and use them to help face temptations.

Chapter 91

TROUBLE

Scott and I went duck hunting and used his three-wheeler. On the way out, he got turned sideways in a mud hole and goosed it trying to get out. When he did, the three-wheeler stood up dumping me out the back and filling my waders with icy water. It took a while sitting in front of the heater in the truck to get comfortable.

Scott and I were in a deer club at Hatley on the Sipsey River close to the MS/AL state line. We both decided to go hunting one morning before daylight. When I got up in the tree, I heard Scott yelling my name. He had gotten off balance and fell out of the tree breaking his ribs. It never hurts to know the location of the nearest hospital.

On another day, Gary and I were hunting the game area. I had a good spot where I was seeing a lot of sign so Gary went to the other side of the road. As happened all too often, he killed a six-point and I didn't see anything. I took the four-wheeler to the deer to get it out. On the way out through a cutover, I ran into a log at an angle. The four-wheeler rolled over going to the right. I jumped and rolled through a briar thicket trying to get away from it. It rolled all the way over upright only bending my gun case. We drove it on out. A man can go through a briar thicket pretty fast if he is scared enough.

It wasn't only on hunting trips where we found trouble. We had a good snow one winter and rigged up something to play in it. We hooked a car hood to the back of Scott's Ford Ranger with a long rope. Three of us could ride on it, but uncomfortably. It was quite exciting until one particular wreck. The snow was about three inches thick with a film of ice on top. The way we wrecked someone said they thought I had figured out a way to snow ski on my head. When I got up, the ice had sliced my head in a circle just like a bowl haircut. The cut was along my temple, so I suppose it did seem like I was skiing on top of my head. We had the same sort of fun with a wheel barrel and the three-wheeler.

Job 14:1 sums it all up: "Man that is born of a woman is of few days, and full of trouble." Our troubles were minor compared to Job's. He is an example of how we should handle times of difficulty.

Chapter 92

REDLAND WATERSHED SURPRISE – LIE

Mitch, Scott, Tonya, and I went fishing at Redland watershed lake. Scott and Tonya fished in a water scamp two-man boat. Mitch and I put a couple of lawn chairs in our ten-foot aluminum boat. We went into a shallow area that was covered in moss. We found a tree stretched out into the water with no moss around it and figured that a big bass must have cleared a spot out where it was bedding. We tried the old faithful plastic worm with no success. Suddenly, something rolled the water. We thought it must have been a huge carp or a beaver. Bubbles started rising through the moss in a four-foot wide trail straight out to our boat. The bubbles went past our boat and on out into the lake about thirty or forty more feet and stopped. A stick appeared where the bubbles stopped. It had knots on both ends. I hadn't noticed it before, so I guessed it was a stick. We decided to paddle toward it and see what it was. As we got closer, we could tell that it wasn't a stick. One of the knots on one end was a big yellow eye with a slanted pupil. The other end was the nose. It flopped again this time almost splashing water on us and headed out toward Scott and Tonya. We never saw it again, but always pondered on catching it somehow. Alligators are not common in this part of Mississippi, so you can imagine our surprise!

Ananias and Sapphira must have been surprised when the apostles knew they had told a lie. It must have surprised everyone else when their punishment was instant and severe. It might be good for all of us to see some instant and severe punishment. "And great fear came upon all the church, and upon as many as heard these things."

—Acts 5:11

Chapter 93

SNEAK ON FIVE DEER
AT NOXUBEE –
HIDE

I was bow hunting and moving a stand to a different spot between Bluff Lake and the Noxubee River on the Noxubee Wildlife Refuge. I saw a couple of deer up in front of me in the woods a hundred-and-fifty or two-hundred yards away. I set the stand down and began the trek toward the deer. I went to the right into some thicker woods down wind of the deer. I was running at a pretty good pace trying to catch up with them, then came to a creek that looked like it veered to the left toward where I thought the deer would be. I got into the creek and started toward the deer.

When I got to where I thought I should be able see them, I found a big Pin Oak tree on the side of the creek. I eased up the edge of the creek behind the tree and peeked around with my left eye. To my surprise, one deer was lying broadside in the leaves about twenty-five yards away, looking directly at me. There were three more deer behind her. I moved back behind the tree and began to draw my bow. It was tricky to draw behind the tree with the bow pointed directly at the ground standing on the side of the creek. I managed to get it drawn and started around the tree with the broadhead showing itself first. When I got my bow completely exposed and the deer in my peepsite, she was looking at me but still lying in the leaves. I estimated thirty yards and released. The arrow sailed true to the five-yard miscalculation right over her back. She jumped up and ran back with the other deer and stopped at about forty-five yards. I hid behind the tree, knocked another arrow, and let it fly. I don't even know which way I missed her that time, but I did.

Occasionally we can hide from a deer without it ever knowing we were around. Jonah tried to hide knowing full well what God wanted him to do. "But Jonah rose up to flee unto Tarsish from the presence of the Lord."

—Jonah 1:3a

Chapter 94

CHICKEN HOUSE
SNOW –
DISCIPLINE

A snow and ice storm caused some damage around the county. A chicken house fell in and we were invited to come and get all the chickens we wanted. We got two dog boxes full of chickens and brought them to the barn. I helped kill the chickens. It didn't happen like the cartoons where the rooster sticks his neck out over the stump and allows you to chop his head off with an axe. We grabbed the chickens two at a time by the head one in each hand. We wrung their necks by swinging them around just like you would a jump rope handle when jumping rope. After we twisted their heads off, they flopped around on the barn floor for a few minutes.

I love to eat chicken just like I am sure many of you do. I think my aunt ended up trashing hers out of the

225

freezer, because of her memories of dressing them. Smile Aunt Vickie, it wasn't that bad!

Those chickens on the barn floor remind me of the way some of our RA boys act on Wednesday night at church. There is not a good way to discipline someone else's children. The most productive options are to hold them out of the activities they enjoy. In some cases Attention Deficit Disorder or ADD could be better described as DDD or Discipline Deficit Disorder. As difficult as it sometimes is, we should let them know that we want them there and make them feel welcome.

I pray for my own kids often and for wisdom in disciplining them. One thing that seemed to work when they were very young was "the bench." When you take a young child out of church because they have misbehaved, it is very important they don't think it is fun. We've taken them to the bench outside the church several times. They must sit there and be still. They have also received a swat or two. I sometimes wonder if a simple whisper "Do you want to go to the bench?" will calm them down when they misbehave after they are in college.

"He that spareth his rod hateth his son: but he that loveth him chasteneth him betimes."
—Proverbs 13:24

Chapter 95

SNAKES AND BEAVER–
PERSPECTIVE

We went gigging and took a bow with us one night behind one of my friend's house in a watershed lake. The lake was shallow and mossy. We kept seeing a huge snake, but never could get a shot at it. We gigged a frog on the bank under some trees. When we went to retrieve it, there was a cottonmouth snake lying within about a foot of the frog. We shot the snake and thought it was such a prize that we put it in the boat with us. We did this again a little while later so we had two snakes tied up with a fish stringer in the boat with us. It was only an eight-foot flat bottom aluminum boat. A living snake in its own habitat looks slick, shiny, mean, and intimidating. A dead snake usually takes a while to stop moving. When the snake slithers around in the boat with you for a while it loses its appeal. I always wondered why we put those snakes in the boat with us.

We saw a beaver once and decided we would try to shoot it with the bow (which had a line and a reel attached). The beaver went under water and we didn't see it until it was almost directly under us. When I drew and tried to get on the beaver, it was already under the boat and moving fast. Standing and moving in an eight-foot boat with two snakes and three more people almost caused me to shoot a hole through the boat. Had we stuck the beaver, I am confident he would have turned the boat over.

When shooting at fish or anything else under the water, the refractory of the light in the water causes the target to appear higher than it is. If you shoot directly at it, your arrow will go over the target. You must shoot low in order to hit it. The depth determines how low.

> Our mind tells us the fish or another target is in a certain place. It is not there! In our daily living we rationalize things to be the way we want them to be or the way the world has told us they should be. We must continually look to the Word for God's perspective.

Chapter 96

CATFISHING TRADITIONS

When we were young, my family and two others always went to South Pontotoc catfishing on the Fourth of July. The fish were hard to catch, but we always caught a few. I remember more about getting my hook hung on stumps than I do about the fish. It wasn't about fishing as much as it was about fellowshipping. My favorite thing to see was always the albino catfish in the tank where we were paying for the fish we caught.

My dad and I went quail hunting on Thanksgiving Day for several years in a row. One of the problems with starting traditions is the disappointment when something happens to end them. I don't think the Pharisees understood when Jesus ended many of their traditions.

"Then the Pharisees and scribes asked him, Why walk not thy disciples according to the tradition of the elders, but eat bread with unwashen hands? He answered and said unto them, Well hath Esaias prophesied of you hypocrites, as it is written, This people honoureth me with their lips, but their heart is far from me"

—Mark 7:5-6

Chapter 97

THE DOVE TREE – PREACH

One year we fixed a dove field behind Mike Bowen's where he had cleared some land. We had a pretty good opening day dove hunt, but I always remember the hunts afterward. One time I went to the field by myself. The trouble with dove hunting by yourself is finding a location where you can shoot them. After hunting a little while, I noticed a tree in the field where a high percentage of the doves were going. It was a dead tree that still had the limbs on it but no leaves. I went to the tree and waited. It wasn't long before I had my limit. Doves are normally very difficult to hit, because they fly so fast. The odds change when they cup their wings and float through the air to land in a tree. It is kind of cool to shoot a dove that is flying toward you, and then stick your hand out and catch it before it hits the ground.

God wants us to keep our eyes focused on Him but to look for the barren limbs where souls are ready for harvest. "And he commanded us to preach unto the people, and to testify that it is he which was ordained of God to be the Judge of quick and dead."

—Acts 10:42

Chapter 98

APPLE ORCHARD
FISHING –
BALANCE

There is a spring fed pond in the back pasture behind my Granny's next to the old apple orchard. The orchard hasn't been there since I was a small child, but once something is known a certain way, something else has to happen to change its name.

The pond had a big bass that lurked around in it. We could see it, but couldn't catch it. There was a lot of brush around the pool and a tree had fallen out into the water off of a high bank. The tree was the best place to fish only because you could walk out on it and be away from the bank far enough to cast. It was only about a foot and a half in diameter. The base end of it was probably eight or ten feet over the water. It wasn't too bad walking out onto the tree, but turning around was a different story.

There were three things that kept peace among friends (or minimized the horseplay): we all wanted to fish off the tree, we knew the fish would be gone for a while if we knocked each other in the water, and snakes. We snuck down to the pool one time to see if the big bass was lurking around the tree, when two snakes came racing across the water like they were fighting. For some reason our desire to catch a fish went away. We left without wetting a hook.

> Balancing on the tree was simple compared to some of the balancing acts that we try today. Between church activities, kids sports, family sickness, and homework, I really enjoy a night when we don't have to be anywhere or do anything. I am not so sure that God meant for us to live life as fast as we do. "Be still, and know that I am God."
>
> —Psalm 46:10a

Chapter 99

SHOOTING TURTLES -
BOREDOM

When hunting season was out and we had fished until we were tired of it, we would break out the 22-calibers and go turtle hunting. Turtles will quickly overpopulate a small pool. There were several small pools where we tried to keep the population in check.

There are good and bad points to shooting into a pond. The bad is the bullet sometimes ricochets off the water. You must know what is behind where you are shooting. The good is you can tell exactly where you hit and compensate for the next shot. A tricky thing about shooting turtles is you must decide whether you are going to shoot at the body of the turtle or the head. The head is usually all you can see. The turtles that pop up close are usually easy to hit if you are fast enough to get the shot off before they see you.

Most of the turtles were terrapin or snapping turtles. They usually ranged in size from a silver dollar to a hubcap. The snapping turtles were good to eat, but quite a lot of trouble. If you were patient and the sun was shining bright enough, the turtles would walk out onto the bank or a log to get some sun. The only time we got those shots was when we were sneaking down to the pool.

I have always hunted and fished for multiple reasons. One of them was because I didn't have anything better to do. Outside is where I feel closest to my Savior. His creation outdoors is closer to the way it was in the beginning.

Solomon shares his wisdom in the book of Ecclesiastes concerning the vain attempts at filling the emptiness in our lives: "One generation passeth away and another generation cometh: but the earth abideth for ever" Ecclesiastes 1:4. If we don't spend our time fearing God and keeping his commandments, then we will come to the same conclusions that Solomon did. "Then I looked on all the works that my hands had wrought, and on the labour that I had laboured to do: and, behold, all was vanity and vexation of spirit, and there was no profit under the sun."
—Ecclesiastes 2:11

Chapter 100

KUDZU – SPREAD

My Granny used to be a firebug; she liked to burn to keep things clean. My dad and my uncle would take the tractor with disc and go around different blocks of woods or pasture and prepare for the big burn. We would then take torches—sometimes made of sage grass—and go around setting fire. We would back burn into the wind so the fire would not spread too rapidly. One time we were burning a block of woods that was filled with kudzu. Kudzu is a rapid growing vine that was introduced here to keep the creek banks from washing away. The kudzu had filled the trees and spread to a point that it was out of control. I think this particular burn was in the spring while the kudzu was still dormant. When the fire went up into the trees in the southeast corner of the property, the blaze must have gone sixty to eighty feet high. I remember sometime during the night, the forestry service showed up in the woods with a dozer and a bunch of firefighters. I don't remember where Granny was, but it seems that my dad and my uncle had a tough time explaining the fire.

It seems there are a lot of similarities between kudzu and the Word—or at least should be!
1) It spreads into places it is not wanted.
2) It clings to things keeping them from washing away.
3) It gets high into the trees and low into the ditches.
4) It only takes a sprig to get started.

Chapter 101

SWEET POTATOES – FOLLOW

In the summer of 2006 we had an unusually long draught. My daughter was playing softball in a neighboring town where I usually get sweet potatoes to feed the deer. I stopped by and bought about a pickup bed load (or about twenty-five bushels) of potatoes. After a week or two, I noticed how much the deer had eaten, so I picked up four more crates or eighty bushels of potatoes. I put three crates onto a sixteen-foot trailer and another crate in the back of my truck. I shoveled them all out within sight of my house and used a spotting scope to watch the deer. The most I saw were five deer at one time, but I have no idea how many were actually eating. They ate all the potatoes in about four weeks time except the half crate that I had left on the trailer. After that I moved the trailer to see if they would eat right out of it. It's hard work shoveling eighty bushels of potatoes out onto the ground! For five out of eight days I saw a seven point with an eleven to twelve inch spread. He had velvet and perfect four points on his right side. The left side looked to be broken off after the second tine. I thought it might still be growing, but it didn't appear any different in the following few days that I watched him.

My sister came over to the house and asked about a little deer in the road. Chet and I and my one-year-old nephew, Jack, went and checked it out. It was a beautiful little spotted fawn about the size of a swamp rabbit. It had been run over some time that morning. It was so beautiful and so small. I thought I could probably wrap my hand all the way around its head.

The draught was forcing deer to move all over to find something to eat and drink. I am sure when the deer saw some of their friends, they brought them to the food. Maybe their friends saw their stomachs were full and decided to follow them around.

When Jesus was gathering his disciples, Andrew brought his brother, Simon Peter, to Jesus. Philip found Nathanael and brought him to Jesus. Following Jesus ultimately resulted in physical death for several of Jesus' disciples. The deer might have gained life-sustaining food by following. Following Jesus may result in some things that are not so pleasant here on this earth. But the peace that passes all understanding and the eternal rewards far outweigh any troubles we face here. "Nathanael answered and saith unto him, Rabbi, thou art the Son of God; thou art the King of Israel."

—John 1:49

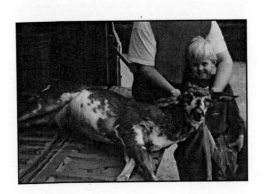

Chapter 102

THE PIEBALD –
FORGIVENESS

My neighbor, J. D. Adams, and I turned the beagles (Loretta and Reba) loose one day. They jumped a deer and made a few rounds before we saw it. The deer jumped out close to J. D. where my garden is currently located. It wasn't very big so he pondered on it and decided to shoot it anyway because it was piebald. He killed it right on the corner of where my shop is now standing. J. D. had somewhere he needed to go, so I skinned the deer. I thought the hide would be neat to have on the wall. The deer had white streaks and spots on his side and on his face. It was an unusually beautiful deer, except for the high crown on the bridge of its nose. I skinned the deer to get the entire hide, except the feet and including the face and ears and nose. It was a lot of trouble to get the hide off the head without cutting it

244

anywhere. I had made a knife out of 440C stainless steel. I remember dropping the knife while I was skinning the deer and breaking the blade. I must have gotten it too hard when I heat treated it.

When I went to pick up the hide from the taxidermist who had sent it off somewhere to be chemically tanned, he said that he had cut the head off of it. He didn't think I wanted the head tanned. I took it anyway but was very upset the head was missing. I spent years thinking no one in their right mind would cut the head off a hide that had been skinned so thoroughly. I even considered whether the head had actually been used to mount a different set of antlers, because of its unusual beauty. I gave the hide to J.D. a couple of years ago. There were two reasons: he had shot it and would enjoy it. Also, I harbored bad feelings that came back whenever I noticed the hide hanging in my shop.

A few months ago, I took my son's first deer hide to get it tanned—to a different taxidermist. Even after specific instructions about getting the head skin tanned also, the hide came back with the head cut off right behind the ears.

I think God was reminding me I did not have the right attitude about the first hide. I don't think I should have forgotten it or necessarily gone back to the same taxidermist. But I should not have let it consume me whenever I looked at the hide. He gives us specific instructions about forgiveness. Jesus told Peter in Matthew 18:22 that we shouldn't forgive someone seven times, but seventy times seven. How many times do we get hung up on one and can't even get to two?

Chapter 103

CHET'S FIRST DEER – BLESSINGS

Chet waved his orange hat to his cousin for all the woods to see and five minutes later two deer fed into the food plot. I advised Chet to take his time because they were a long ways off, but feeding our way. When we looked up they were gone. I wanted to kick myself; I had thought they were too far at about one hundred and ninety yards.

We were hunting on my brother's property where he had used a dozer to clear off a large food plot in the middle of a pine cutover in the New Hope community in Pontotoc. Deer were keeping the rye grass and oats mowed down to the ground so we were confident in seeing one. We were in a four by four shooting house with no roof and no side on one side. It had a slot for shooting on the side where the deer had come out that was about three by ten inches. The slot was close to the perfect height for Chet to stand and shoot from. Reset pines were small enough that we could see the shooting house on the next ridge where my brother, Barry, and his daughter, Maggie, were.

I enjoyed seeing the lake below us with ducks flying in and out. Chet was much more interested in seeing Maggie and her seeing us than he was hunting. He had a 7600 Remington 243 pump rifle in the corner of the shooting house where we were sitting in lawn chairs.

Just before dark, two more deer came out in the same place or maybe they were the same deer. I told Chet to go for it. He eased the gun barrel out the slot. I peered through the edge trying to see. He squeezed off a shot and the deer jumped straight up in the air. He tried to pump another shell in the chamber and couldn't get it to go, so he handed me the gun. I put another round in the barrel and handed it back to him. He took another shot. We handed off through seven shots, the last one hit the deer's head at one hundred and eighty yards. He hit it four out of seven times with it almost dark at the end of the food plot. Some time in the middle of the shooting his Uncle Barry came on the radio and asked what was going on. Uncle Barry smeared a little blood on Chet's jaws to cap off the experience.

Acts 20:35 says that it is more blessed to give than to receive. Barry and I got more joy out of the hunt than Chet, even though he was the one doing the shooting. Sometimes I think my kids have been spoiled about hunting and don't appreciate it. Take a kid hunting that doesn't belong to you and doesn't get a chance to go. See if you can instill in him or her a love for it like you have. I can't think of many better things for a kid to get addicted to.

The blessings aren't so easy to see when we are helping others under certain conditions. There is always a "no monetary return" policy or it wouldn't be giving. Sometimes there is no appreciation. Sometimes no one ever even knows. These are the times when I think we are building up treasures in heaven. "But lay up for yourselves treasures in heaven, where neither moth nor rust doth corrupt, and where thieves do not break through nor steal."

—Matthew 6:20

Chapter 104

MUSHROOMS – LIFE FOR LIFE

Chet and I were hunting on CL hunting club when we noticed some mushrooms growing in an oval pattern about three or four feet across and two feet wide at the edge of some hardwoods. We stopped and looked, and then pondered on it for quite a while that afternoon. Did something give up its life allowing the mushrooms to live?

I have been studying about mushrooms a little and actually ate a few puffballs that I gathered around the house. It was against the wishes of my family who wouldn't taste them until the second or third day, because they wanted to make sure I didn't die from eating poisonous mushrooms. When I cut them open, they looked like a fresh loaf bread on the inside. They were delicious. I think anything can be made to taste good if you batter it in flour and fry it in bacon grease. In my mind I kept going back to the pattern that the mushrooms were growing in. If given the opportunity, I will study it a little closer next time.

> When we think of losing life to gain it, I always go back to the Savior. Christ came and gave his life so that we might have life eternal.
>
> —John 3:16

Chapter 105

DOUBLE ARMADILLO STINK

One time, Jan woke me up—or tried to—at two or three o'clock in the morning. She said something had killed Buck Owens (our beagle). She thought it was an armadillo and it was on the back porch. I remember thinking that as long as someone wasn't breaking into our house, it would be okay until the dawn.

The next morning, I was looking out the back window and noticed a tail sticking out of the swimming pool skimmer. I then remembered the conversation. Rusty the bloodhound and Buck had tore the top off the skimmer trying to get to the armadillo and it was wedged in the skimmer slot. I used a ball bat to try and get it out. I got it back into the water where it began swimming around the pool. Rusty was trying to grab it with his mouth to get it out like he normally does snakes and mice. His problem was getting his mouth around it because it was about eight or ten inches in diameter. Every time Rusty would grab for its head, it would suck its head back down into its shell.

I then noticed another armadillo in the other skimmer. It must have been an exciting night. I tried getting on my knees so I could grab the armadillo by the tail and sling it out, but Rusty was going to push me in. He wasn't doing it on purpose; he just didn't want to move away from it himself. I used the pool sweeper to get it up so that Rusty could grab it. He got it around the bottom of its shell and snatched it out. Then I went to the other skimmer where the other one had climbed all the way in and just wasn't coming out. I used the bat for a little while trying to get it out with no success. I then tried to coax Rusty into getting it out for me. He was occupied and didn't want to leave the other one. I reached down, grabbed it by the ears, and yanked it out. It ran over toward the house with Buck close behind it. I caught up with it close to the back porch and popped it with the ball bat. Rusty then saw there was more going on and joined in. Unfortunately, I had to leave for work. When I got home, I told the kids to go find the armadillos so we could get rid of them before they started stinking. They couldn't find them.

Three days later Jan was planting flowers in front flower bed and decided she either needed a bath desperately or something was dead. She had found one of them. A few days later I found the other one on the outside of the underground fence. There was nothing left except a clean shell. Something must have eased up into Rusty and Buck's patrol area and dragged it away for an evening snack. I have found opossums and raccoons in the yard before that had ventured into their domain. I wonder if we will find a fox, bobcat, or coyote next? I am sure it will be a much more interesting fight. It might even wake me up.

Sometimes it is amazing how God allows us to hear some things and not others. I am a heavy sleeper and can sleep through almost anything. When my son was about two years old, I heard him say "Daddy" twice in the middle of the night. I got up and went into his room to check on him. He wasn't there. I went down the hall into the living room and kitchen and began to get frantic. The door was cracked open into the carport. When I looked out, Chet was there; he had walked out into the rain, and then turned back into the carport. When he couldn't get the storm door open, he said he began calling for me. Hearing Chet call me in the middle of the night, on the other end of the house, outside, with it raining has always seemed to me as one of God's tiny miracles.

After three days there were maggots and a very strong smell associated with the armadillo. In John 11:39 Martha told Jesus that Lazarus "stinketh" because he had been dead four days. Jesus then performed a miracle. Later Jesus was crucified and then resurrected on the third day. "Then arose Peter, and ran unto the sepulcher; and stooping down, he beheld the linen clothes laid by themselves, and departed, wondering in himself at that which was come to pass" Luke 24:12. I wonder if the clothes and tomb had the smell of death or of life?

Chapter 106

JAN'S CATFISH

My daughter, Cailey, had named a catfish in my Granny's pond *Goliath*. We had hamburgers for lunch at the pond one time on the Saturday before Memorial Day, 2005. Daddy had bought a trailer truck load of sand and dumped it in a huge pile beside the water. The kids had played in it all day on Friday and thought they had to go back on Saturday. Chet, Cailey, Maggie, Sloan, and Max worked as hard as they could digging holes and filling them with water, then filling them back in with sand. An umbrella duct taped to a hoe handle and stuck up in the sand made it look like a real beach. Jack and Molly just enjoyed from the sideline.

Daddy and Barry made their way around the pool catching a few small bass. Jan decided she wanted to fish as well. I got her a spinning reel that had a large jig on it with no grub. I put two plastic grubs on the hook, because I didn't want to tie anything else on the line. I was going to put a plastic worm on the hook but couldn't find one. She went fishing. I grabbed a rod that had a plastic worm on it and went around the pool fishing myself. I was soon alarmed by the shrieking on the other side of the pool." I got one—it's a big one, it's a big one!" Jan had caught the lunker of the day on the ridiculous rig I had given her. I would have been surprised if it had caught a bass and much more so a catfish. I guess I shouldn't have been surprised, because Chet had fished for a while the day before with nothing but a rock and almost caught one. Probably the same catfish had lunged at the rock and startled him as Chet was taking it out of the water. I know you are wondering about it. Yes, it is quite difficult to tie a rock onto a line where it won't throw off. Oh, and you can see Max in the picture with his pullup on. The sand forced him to come out of the pullup. He enjoyed the afternoon playing in the sand and water in his birthday suit.

Tying a rock onto a fishing line is not a very productive way to catch fish, and we can draw some parallels to our spiritual life:
- If we don't get a secure and confident education in God's Word, that education won't be there when we need it. The physical rock won't be there for many casts.

- We are fishing for men (and women) but not really expecting to catch anything.
- We are not ready to help when God draws a person to himself; we can't set the hook because with a rock there is no hook.
- We are just fishing to look like we are fishing or to say we are fishing or just to kill time. Surely a person fishing with a rock knows he/she isn't going to catch anything.
- The fish might bite the rock, but it will spit it out before it drags him out of the water. If we aren't living for God, then our friends who are considering accepting Christ see us as a reason not to.

My prayer is this last thought burdens you as it does me to live for Christ.

Chapter 107

CAILEY'S FIRST DOVE –
BELIEVE

O n opening weekend of dove season 2006, Cailey, Chet, and I picked up one of Chet's buddies and went dove hunting at my dad's wheat and rye grass field that he plants for his horses. Cailey and Daddy set up lawn chairs within shooting distance of an Oak tree where the doves like to land. Chet, Austin, and I went to the blind in the middle of the field, but had two guns among the three of us; I thought that would be easier to manage with two young hunters.

The two boys could hear Cailey shooting and every once in a while would see a bird fall in her direction. They were sweating the possibility she might harvest more birds than them. They had even made up a story about how many they had killed before they even put one in the bucket. The way Cailey explained it, she got one when it was flying out of the tree. If she had only thought about it, she could have had those two boys going with just a little trickery.

As the early morning sun starts to burn away the darkness, a first bird always floats in. And it almost never fails, when shooting at the first bird, the fire coming out the end of the barrel always catches my attention. When I see it, I always wonder why I never notice it at other times. Is it possible that early in the morning something is burning that doesn't in the daytime? I think not. I think some of the powder doesn't completely burn until the wadding is out of the end of the barrel. It is just not easy to see in the daytime, because the light around it is more intense. Does this mean it is not there if we can't see it in the daytime?

Cailey and I went back hunting that evening. It didn't take long to realize she was fast on the trigger. She reminded me of *Trinity* (if he had used a shotgun) in my favorite old western. At the end of the day she got on the four-wheeler and followed Granddaddy to the house, which was okay except she forgot to come back and get me. It didn't take me long to realize I had been left behind.

When the Lord comes back to take his own, I think some folks will know immediately what has happened, but others will have to figure it out. We don't physically see Christ every day, but he is always with us. When Thomas doubted, Jesus said, "Reach hither thy finger, and behold my hands; and reach hither thy hand, and thrust it into my side: and be not faithless, but believing. And Thomas answered and said unto him, My Lord and my God. Jesus saith unto him, Thomas, because thou hast seen me, thou hast believed: blessed are they that have not seen, and yet have believed."

—John 20:27-29

Chapter 108

A FAVORITE RECIPE

My kids' favorite food is deer meat—fried. When my daughter was about four-years-old, I told her there was a deer standing in the back yard. She leaned over the back of the couch looking and commented, "Mmmm, deer meat!"

Ingredients: 3/8-inch thick deer steaks; self rising flour; salt and pepper; corn oil

Short recipe: Tenderize the meat; wet the meat with water then drop in flour getting a good coat; fry in oil on medium.

There are several little tricks to making fried deer steaks that the kids love. I will start from the beginning.

In the south, we don't always have the luxury of hanging the deer outside for a few days. I prefer to fillet the meat off the bones after skinning the deer, then cover the meat in ice in a cooler. I pour the water off and add ice about every day or every other day for seven to nine days.

The inside tenderloins and the backstraps are the best cuts. But, properly prepared, there are a lot of other muscles just as good. I separate the muscles and cut away everything white. I then cross cut the muscle into 3/8-inch thick steaks. I use a tenderizing hammer to pulverize the meat. The edge of a plastic plate works well, but takes a little longer. The more it is hammered the more tender the meat will become. If cutting up an entire deer, I like to put the cut steaks in the refrigerator and stir and change the water for three or four days before freezing. This gives more time for the blood to drain from the meat. After tenderizing, the meat should be put back in water before battering. To batter, I use flour only. I know this sounds simple, but I have tried a lot of other mixtures with limited success. Plain self-rising flour is always liked the best. A stove top skillet with an eighth to a quarter-inch of corn oil must reach temperature on medium before putting the meat in. If the oil is not hot, the flour will not stick to the meat very well. When the blood comes to the top and the edge has started turning brown, it is time to flip the meat. The most common mistake in cooking deer meat is overcooking; it is tricky to get the batter crisp without overcooking it. Overcooking will make it tougher.

Practice makes perfect. After taking the meat out of the oil and placing on paper towels for draining, add salt and pepper to taste.

> I go to a lot of trouble to make deer taste good. Esau must have as well. It was his father's dying wish to have some. "And he said, behold now, I am old, I know not the day of my death: Now therefore take, I pray thee, thy weapons, thy quiver and thy bow, and go out to the field, and take me some venison; And make me some savory meat, such as I love, and bring it to me, that I may eat; that my soul may bless thee before I die."
>
> —Genesis 27:2-4

Isaac and Esau both had issues with food. Esau sold his birthright for a bowl of soup. Isaac wanted the venison to help get himself in the mood to give the blessing to Esau. Genesis 25:28 said that Isaac loved Esau, because he did eat of his venison. Did he chose which son he liked best, because of the food they cooked? We should be careful not to condemn their actions without analyzing the decisions we make with reference to food.

Chapter 109

MY TESTIMONY

I was brought up in a Christian home. As a very small child, my cousin and I asked Jesus into our hearts bunches of times, but I thought it couldn't be that simple. When I was seven-years-old, I attended a Wednesday night prayer meeting where Brother Jack Gregory showed a film that had something to do with "fire insurance." It was about hell. On the way home from church, in the back of the big blue four-door car that my family owned, I invited Christ into my life and he saved me. I had some doubts for a couple of years, but I was baptized at age nine. Something about baptism gave me an assurance I had not felt before then. Maybe it had something to do with confessing Jesus before others as is mentioned in Romans 10:9, 10. It also could have been that peaceful feeling that comes with being obedient.

God kept me safe from trouble all through school. In most cases, he kept evils from even tempting me when a lot of the people around me were very tempted. Without his arms around me, I am sure things would have been a lot different in college.

God blessed me with Jan who is a wonderful mother and could not be more loving and kind. He also blessed me with two wonderful kids. We had to put the first one into his hands at an early age. When Chet was born, he was diagnosed with congenital heart disease. The first doctor we spoke with said, "There might be a child somewhere in the world that had lived through what he has." You can imagine the devastation. The next doctor said he has fixed this problem every day. The roller coaster ride had begun. As Chet was rolled to open heart surgery with big bright eyes wide open and looking at us, the strangest sense of who was in control overpowered me. As an engineer, I sometimes convince myself that I am in control. I think God uses my kids to regularly remind me that he is in control.

If you haven't committed yourself to Christ and invited him into your life, I invite you to do so today. The excitement of the hunt and the thrill of the outdoors are magnificently enhanced by a personal relationship with the Creator of it all. Whether you are old or young, you can spend the rest of your life walking and talking with him—and then for eternity.

Pleasant
Word

LaVergne, TN USA
19 May 2010
183310LV00002B/1/P